Scenery, space, and the human connection: an illustrated guide. There is probably nothing that has influenced the Japanese garden more than the love the Japanese people have always had for their landscape. The first color photograph in this book shows one of Japan's "Three Great Views," the pineclad islands of Matsushima Bay off Shiogama on the northeast coast. In olden days, with changes in the distribution of property, aristocrats began to journey far from the capital of Kyoto to look after their holdings in the hinterlands. For many it was their first time away from home, and they delighted in the natural beauty of the archipelago as they traveled its coasts and waters. Matsushima Bay was one of the favorite panoramas and was often celebrated in verse. One man in the ninth century, the emperor's Minister of the Left, Minamoto no Tōru, admired the view so much that he attempted to evoke it on the grounds of his own urban Kyoto estate using a pond, stones, and plantings. The minister's garden no longer exists, but the impulse to re-create and celebrate the world of nature is still an

essential starting point for Japanese garden design. ● Intimacy with nature has to do with recognition of nature's bounty and reverence for its indwelling forces. The very earliest "gardens" in Japan, produced by a simple society that relied on the natural environment for its sustenance, may have been just clearings in the forest, marked off and spread with white gravel so that the gods—called *kami*—of the trees and mountains would have a place to manifest themselves. A more developed form of this sanctified zone appears in the next color photo. This is Takihara Shrine, 40 kilometers southwest of the larger Ise Shrine complex dedicated to the ancestral gods of the imperial family. As at Ise, every twenty years the Takihara Shrine is razed, while another identical building is erected on an adjacent piece of land. A pillar from the old shrine remains in the empty zone until the new shrine is knocked down twenty years later and reconstruction begins anew. The open area and the rebuilding ceremony represent purity and the forces of renewal: both are an intrinsic part of the Japanese view of nature and distinguish it from Christian and Buddhist cosmologies. ● If gods

text by **Teiji Itoh**

are immanent in nature, the whole world is a garden. Perhaps only this expansive notion could explain the scene in the next photograph, the Upper Villa of the Shugakuin Detached Palace, a garden built by the retired emperor Gomizuno-o in the seventeenth century. The spacious Pond of the Bathing Dragon is entirely manmade—the bank on the opposite shore was constructed as a dam. Beyond are the hills to the north and west of Kyoto. What joins this garden to the distant scenery is the overarching sky. In other words, the cloud-filled dome is part of the garden, as much so as the pond. People often say the Japanese garden represents miniaturization, but this is the reverse—an attempt to expand the garden to almost cosmic proportions. ● Shugakuin's strength and spectacle, however, are at one extreme within the Japanese tradition. The next photographs show how nature is made intimate by man's design. At Ritsurin Park, in Shikoku in southern Japan, three large rounded stones gently guide the

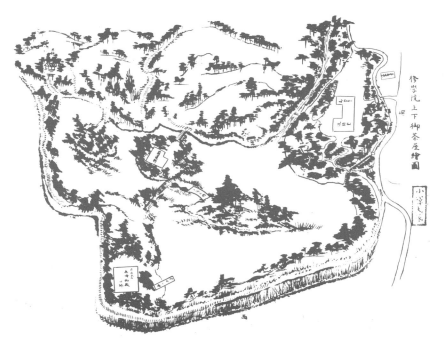

Kodansha International
Tokyo, New York, San Francisco

DENS

eye from a shoreline onto the water's surface and across to a graceful bridge. This garden was completed in 1744 and was the property of the Matsudairas, feudal lords of the region, before it passed into public hands. While built on the grand scale—the Matsudairas were very powerful—the garden is quite elegant and a popular place to take a leisurely stroll, with numerous ponds, paths, a pavilion of historical importance, and views of the surrounding hillsides. ● Following is a stone pavement at Katsura Detached Palace. Katsura is an architectural/garden complex in Kyoto, built as a villa for the Hachijō imperial princes about the same time as Shugakuin. But where Shugakuin exploits the space overhead, Katsura (its own fine views notwithstanding) is full of

interest at ankle-level. It has footpaths of astounding variety, many of them so difficult to navigate that the eyes don't dare wander. Detailing throughout, as on the path shown here, is of a complexity that teases the mind. Some critics, however, say that all this makes Katsura too intellectual, too busy. ● Gardens for strolling like Ritsurin Park or Katsura rely on motion. Views appear and disappear, and if the designer was of a playful disposition the garden will be full of tension and surprise. Suddenly, turning a corner, you lift your head to see where you are and there's a perfect view across a pond, or a red-leafed maple in autumn. Other gardens, particularly those developed from the tradition of Zen Buddhist meditation, are meant to be viewed from a seated, stationary position. Such a garden belongs to the temple Entsū-ji, in northern Kyoto, and appears in the next frame. The Entsū-ji garden is a striking example of the technique

OF JA

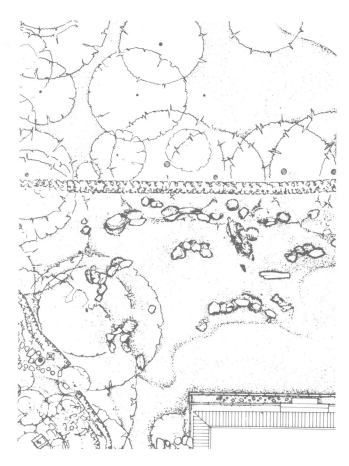

of "borrowed scenery" and the conceptual illusions of Japanese garden design. The figure of Mount Hiei rises far off in the east, but so artfully is its shape counterpointed by the interior stones and plantings that it feels more a part of the garden proper than even the straight hedge and tree trunks that frame it in the middle ground. Recently, there is talk of putting up a tall hotel nearby that will intrude on this composed landscape. The temple strongly objects—the garden they could move, the mountain never, and by now, after all these centuries, the two are wholly symbiotic. ● In the next photograph we again see a framing technique, but this time it uses the wooden pillars of a manmade structure. The garden belongs to the temple Sanpō-in in the countryside southeast of Kyoto. It was begun in 1598 under the instruction of the all-powerful warlord

of the time, Hideyoshi, who did not live to see it completed. The Sanpō-in grounds have been called the Japanese garden gone rococo, and the lavish rockwork is indeed ostentatious by Japanese standards. Traditional Japanese temple architecture uses broad verandas and removable outside walls to integrate interior and exterior spaces. This style probably developed from the hot and humid Japanese summer, but it has attained a level of great aesthetic sophistication. Many Japanese gardens, like Sanpō-in, literally begin within the buildings that overlook them. Or perhaps the buildings begin in the gardens. ● A case in point is the Hayashiya Residence in the next

APAN

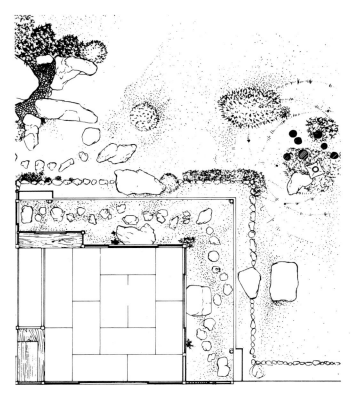

photograph, located in the old castle town of Kanazawa on Japan's north coast. The typical wooden veranda has been replaced by an earthen corridor with plantings, moss, and low-lying stepping stones. Again, climate provides a clue to this construction. In Kanazawa the winter snows can be heavy. The outer railing between the main garden and the corridor can be fitted with doors to seal off the house, leaving this green zone for the enjoyment of family members. ● The Japanese garden moves fully into the house in the next photograph. In a narrow courtyard of the

CONTENTS

Kuwata Residence in Hiroshima, designer Shigemori Mirei has built an expansive universe. Swept white gravel represents the sea, while stones thrust up their bulk in imitation of forested mountains. This garden has enormous motion, so much so that a long slab of cut stone has been placed in the foreground, like a bass accompaniment, to steady the rhythm. The slab consciously imitates the line of the veranda, and by this technique funnels the energies of the garden directly into the home. A composition like this can be overpowering. It intrudes on the mind and the spirit. Built in 1957, this microcosmic space is the culmination of a long tradition of garden-making designed to

stimulate contemplation of the world and the nature of life. ● Now reverse figure and ground. The next photograph shows part of Furumine Shrine in Ibaragi Prefecture, just north of Tokyo. Here in this near-wilderness it is the building that attains a micro-scale. And yet within the clay wall that surrounds this structure—called the Hōshō-an—there is an extensive manicured garden, replete with stone groupings, lanterns, basins, and an exquisite groundcover of lush green moss. Inside and outside zones are demarcated by the wall, but at the same time are interfused by a forest of majestic cypress trees. Designer Iwaki Sentarō says that he built this garden to bring out the beauty of nature. Couldn't he have simply left nature here as it was? The panorama of Matsushima Bay in the first photograph has been much admired by the Japanese over the centuries, but the spacious landscape in itself has never had as much appeal as the same landscape re-created in the space of a garden. Just as the early Japanese created purified zones of white gravel to receive the immanent gods, so does the Japanese gardener create a special median zone that partakes both of man, by virtue of its spatial design, and of nature, by virtue of its materials. It is reasonable to ask whether a garden in the wilderness would exist if there was no one there to see it.

Distributed in the United States by Kodansha International/ USA Ltd., through Harper & Row, Publishers, Inc. 10 East 53rd Street, New York, New York 10022. Published by Kodansha International Ltd., 12-21 Otowa 2-chome, Bunkyo-ku, Tokyo 112 and Kodansha International/USA Ltd., with offices at 10 East 53rd Street, New York, New York 10022 and The Hearst Building, 5 Third Street, Suite 430, San Francisco, California 94103.

First edition, 1984
Second printing, 1984

The main text is a translation from the Japanese and is published here for the first time in any language. All captions for photographs and illustrations were prepared by the editors. Other acknowledgments, notes, and credits appear separately at the end of the book. NOTE: Except for on the title page and in the Bibliography, Japanese names are given in customary Japanese order, surname preceding given name.

Library of Congress Cataloging in Publication Data

Itō, Teiji, 1922– / The gardens of Japan. / Bibliography: p. / Includes index. / 1. Gardens, Japanese. / 2. Gardens— Japan. / I. Title.   SB458.I833 1984 / 712'.0952 / 83-48882
ISBN 0-87011-648-7
ISBN 4-7700-1148-2 (in Japan)

SPLENDID MISINTERPRETATIONS

In primitive times, the people of Japan must have had their own kinds of gardens. We can assume this because we know that, at the dawn of Japanese history, the word *niwa* was used to mean garden and because this same word persists today side by side with the Sino-Japanese term *teien*. The heart of the Japanese garden in its most developed form was in fact the interplay and interaction of the indigenous *niwa* and imported Chinese and Buddhist cultural elements. The point of departure for this study, however, is the degree of faithfulness with which the Japanese translated these borrowed ideas about gardens into native terms.

With some few exceptions, the translations were far from literal and direct. In the front gardens of palaces dating from the fifth and sixth centuries, when the Yamato clan chiefs first imposed a rough political unity over the Japanese islands, were to be found certain kinds of stone sculpture, some of which survive to the present. We still find in the Asuka and Nara regions, for example, stone fountains and standing male and female figures in postures of embrace. But these sculptures seem too decidedly alien to have been Japanese in inspiration; it is likely that immigrants from the Korean peninsula created and installed them as direct cultural translations. They were not appreciated for very long, however, and such direct borrowings soon ceased.

In the eighth and ninth centuries, the Japanese began to misinterpret imported garden culture by deliberately or accidentally ignoring the basic philosophical concepts on which it rested. Viewed unfavorably, this trend can be condemned as a refusal to understand the cultural essences involved; in a positive light, it can be regarded as a way of preserving an independent identity.

The work and thought of Tachibana no Toshitsuna (mid-eleventh century) provides an excellent example of the kind of misinterpretation that was taking place at the time. Toshitsuna was the half-brother of Fujiwara no Yorimichi (990–1074), regent and chief advisor to the emperor; his connections on his mother's side, however, were too lowly to permit his making a name for himself in politics, and he turned instead to a cultural career—notably garden design, in which he attained preeminence. His book on gardening, *Sakutei-ki*, the oldest surviving Japanese text on the topic, contains an illuminating passage on *fengshui*, the geomantic philosophy imported from China. *Fengshui*—literally, "wind and water"—devised spatial layouts on the basis of directions, each of which had its own characteristics

Stone fountain with non-Japanese faces, discovered near Nara. Ca. 7th century

Lake Center Pavilions at Chengde Imperial Summer Resort, northern China.

and influences on human affairs, and is thought to have been introduced into Japan in the sixth century. It must have shocked the Japanese people, who until then had conceived of such things only in terms of inside and outside. No doubt they would never have dreamed of conforming the original universal order to an artificial, manmade order in the way the *fengshui* system does; with only their indigenous magical approaches to the mysteries of the world, they must have found this system all the more puzzling.

Fengshui establishes certain criteria for the desirable sites of palaces, residences, and cemeteries. Tachibana no Toshitsuna mentions them in his text. "Geomantically," he writes, "the best site is one that has a river on the east, a pond on the south, a highway on the west, and a hill on the north because these things correspond to certain divine creatures. The stream corresponds to a blue dragon, the pond to a crimson bird, the highway to a white tiger, and the hill to a black turtle." All of these divine creatures were considered auspicious and capable of conveying health and longevity. Up to this point, Toshitsuna's explanation is identical with the Chinese, but he soon diverges from it. If such a site is unobtainable, he says, one may substitute nine willow trees for the river, nine Judas trees for the pond, seven maple trees for the highway, and three cypress trees for the hill.

The Japanese interpretation, substituting trees for the elements demanded in *fengshui*, meant that any site at all could be safely used for palaces, residences, and cemeteries. The Chinese system has been modified out of all recognition. Probably the ancient Japanese belief that gods dwell in trees helped give rise to this distortion—or, as I have called it, splendid misinterpretation—which enabled the Japanese people to assimilate an alien culture in the creation of a truly native kind of garden. Toshitsuna and others engaged in the same kind of thought and design worked out a philosophy that, while appearing to be *fengshui*, was actually of an entirely different kind.

Cultural influences are sometimes brought in by the sword; sometimes they represent borrowings from advanced cultures on the part of those less developed. Both kinds of influences have impinged upon Japan. With nothing beyond it to the east but the Pacific Ocean, the Japanese archipelago became a kind of final destination where cultural influences from the Asian mainland tended to pile up. In

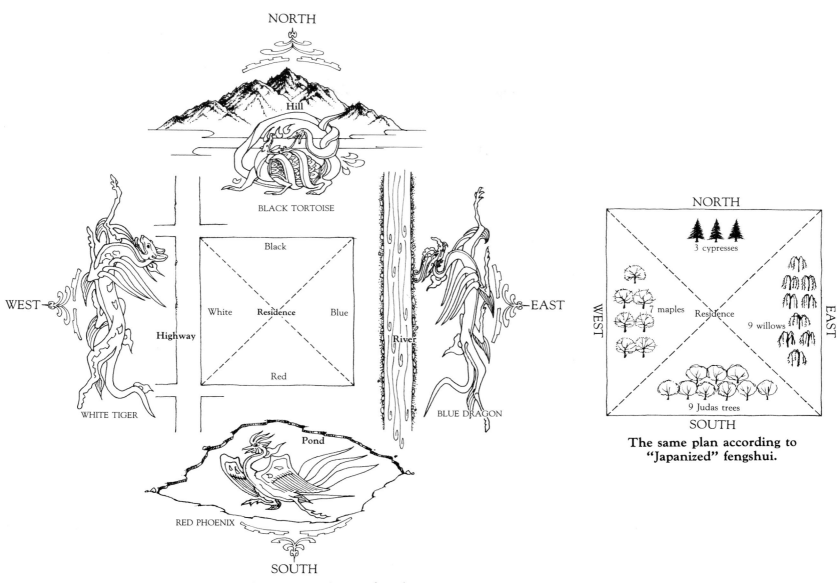

Chinese residential plan according to fengshui.

The same plan according to "Japanized" fengshui.

the sixth century, political unification under a firm central authority was necessary if Japan was to protect itself from foreign threats; still underdeveloped, Japan was compelled at the same time to borrow cultural elements from the more advanced mainland. Among these were Taoism and Buddhism, introduced from China by way of Korea; both influenced native ideas on gardening, but we must keep in mind that there was a relation between the imported and the domestic: foreign ideas did not obliterate indigenous garden forms.

While there was no strong reaction against imported ideas, the native tradition showed no signs of trying to evolve a new, single, eclectic garden form. What path, then, did Japanese garden designers and philosophers take? They chose, as I have indicated, to misinterpret—to allow distorted versions of foreign ideas to exist side by side with primitive, indigenous garden forms.

Sometimes in the design of garden spaces it was essential for the sake of creative focus to find a design source. Here, too, as the following illustrates, the Japanese chose the way of misinterpretation. Between 794 and 1333 (the Heian and Kamakura periods), gardens were frequently created in what was called the Pure Land (or Paradise) style because they were supposed to be earthly representations of Sukhavati, the Western Paradise of the Buddha Amitābha (or Amida, as he is known in Japan). These gardens were favored by the emperor, his consort, the already weakening aristocracy, and the warrior-aristocrats, whose belligerent calling often put their fates in doubt from one day to the next. They reached their pinnacle of popularity in the eleventh and twelfth centuries, when earthquakes, famine, and internal warfare truly made even the immediate future an uncertainty. Unable to formulate effective economic and political policies, the aristocrats

Phoenix Hall at Byōdō-in, Uji.

(nominally still the ruling class) elected to reproduce on earth the beautiful halls and gardens of the Buddhist paradise, where they could achieve the stability that otherwise eluded them. The widespread belief that the year 1051 ushered in the Latter Day of the Law (or Mappō era), when the historical Buddha Shakyamuni had prophesied that Buddhism would be destroyed, probably contributed to this escapist attitude.

At his villa in Uji, not far from the capital city, Kyoto, the great imperial advisor Fujiwara no Yorimichi built such a Pure Land garden. So famous was it for its splendor and beauty that people of the time said anyone who wanted a vision of paradise must see the temple at Uji. Today the temple is called the Byōdō-in, and its most famous attraction is the Amida chapel known as the Phoenix Hall.

In strictly religious terms, the Pure Land is a place to which the faithful dead are conducted by the Buddha Amida himself, who appears to them accompanied by princely clad bodhisattvas riding on many-colored clouds and playing celestial music. However founded they were in religious ideas, the paradise gardens made on Japanese soil by aristocrats like Fujiwara no Yorimichi were actually attempts at an earthly paradise where human beings could submerge themselves in aesthetic pursuits. In short, like Tachibana no Toshitsuna's substitution of trees for the elements of *fengshui*, these gardens constituted misinterpretations of a basic idea.

In their creation, some kind of model was essential, since no living being has ever seen a paradise. The model was found in the images called *mandala*, used by esoteric Buddhist sects to represent the truths of the universe and by other Buddhist sects to convey the appearance of the Western Paradise of Amida. Some of these mandala are quite large; they are often on paper or silk and, in scroll form,

Section of Seikai mandala.

are considered objects of religious veneration. The so-called Seikai mandala (996) bears a striking resemblance to the layout of the Byōdō-in.

The brightly colored Seikai mandala is named for the Buddhist priest Seikai (?–1017), a contemporary of Fujiwara no Michinaga (966–1027)—the father of Fujiwara no Yorimichi—and is counted among the three great examples of the genre in Japan. It shows, in addition to the Buddha Amida himself: a two-story tower; outlying buildings to the right and left connected to the tower by means of arched bridges; an island where peacocks frolic; a pure, cool lake made of the Seven Precious Substances and graced with lotuses in flower; a stage where two boys dance; and a host of bodhisattvas mounted on clouds floating in air. Today, all that remains at the Byōdō-in are a version of the tower in the form of the hall housing a large gilded statue of Amida—the Phoenix Hall, or Hōōdō—and the pond in front. Nonetheless, in the evening, when the tourists have departed and the lamps are alight, the golden statue gleams through the open portals; the reflection of the building in the mirrorlike water of the pond gives us a hint of how the paradise gardens of the past must have looked.

Once again, if not out-and-out misinterpretation, at least considerable latitude of interpretation has been called into play in this garden ensemble. The Seikai mandala can have been no more than an idea source for the layout of the Byōdō-in since it would be impossible to reproduce exactly the fantastic glories of the painting. Yorimichi had his Byōdō-in designed and built to suit his own inclinations. For him, the religious ideas involved were only a means to the achievement of his own ends: rebirth in paradise after death and the creation of a world where he could indulge in aesthetic pursuits while he lived.

EMPTY SPACE AND WHITE GRAVEL

The two most outstanding buildings in the Kyoto Imperial Palace are the great hall of state, called the Shishinden, and the residential and ceremonial banquet hall called the Seiryōden. On the south, or front, side of the former, flanking the main flight of steps leading to the veranda, are a mandarin orange tree on the west and a cherry tree on the east. To the right and left of the flight of steps on the east side of the Seiryōden are small fenced enclosures planted with bamboo trees. Aside from this minimal vegetation, the remaining large spaces—in the case of the Shishinden, quite vast—in front of the buildings are totally empty and spread with white gravel. There is a narrow water channel immediately in front of the Seiryōden, but it is an exception to the otherwise all-prevailing emptiness. Practically all histories of the subject consider this empty, gravel-spread space at the Kyoto Imperial Palace to be one of the primal sources of the Japanese garden.

Interestingly enough, primitive Japanese religious tradition held that divine spirits reside in trees. If this is the case, it would seem an excellent idea to plant as many trees as possible instead of leaving immense areas open. Do spaces of this kind reject or ignore that primitive religious belief?

In a diary entitled *Goshō nikki*, Matsuoka Yukiyoshi (d. 1848) makes this remark on the subject:

> Ōmura Kazusanosuke often mentioned to me a point he considered quite remarkable in connection with the garden: "From ancient times, at imperial palaces, the areas in front of such state halls as the Shishinden and such banquet buildings as the Seiryōden have lacked artificial hillocks and bodies of water and have been spread with white gravel and left otherwise empty. Later, in the time of the Tokugawa shogunate, the areas in front of the great *shoin* halls of official residences—whether the wood was lacquered black or left unpainted—were spread with gravel and left empty of everything but a few trees. They too had neither artificial hillocks nor streams. It seems then that hills, plants, and natural scenes were not re-created in the garden spaces in front of buildings where official functions took place but in front of the living quarters of unofficial buildings, where the residents could take their morning and evening leisure looking at the

garden and writing or reciting poetry." To this I replied that the open spaces before such buildings as banquet halls and the Shishinden were the scenes of official ceremonies attended by great numbers of ministers and court officials there to pay homage to the emperor. There is no room in such a setting for hillocks, streams, or the other elements of the natural scenic garden. Since official functions were not held at detached palaces like the Suzakuin and the Shinsen'en, they invariably incorporated reproductions of natural scenery. Similarly, the residences of people of lower than ministerial rank, since no great ceremonies were held in them either, usually had natural-style front gardens for the delectation of the master of the house and his guests.

Matsuoka's reply seems to me to describe correctly the situation from the dawn of the historical period to the present. Ceremonies marking the investiture of the empress Meishō (1623–96), for example, held in the great foreground of the Shishinden at the Kyoto Imperial Palace, indicate how out of place ponds and hills would be on such occasions. Seven banners about 15 meters tall and five halberds were set up for the ceremony, which was attended by a throng of court aristocrats and representatives of the Tokugawa shogunal government.

Sei Shōnagon, the writer best known for her miscellany *Makura no sōshi* (The Pillow Book), served until her death at the early age of twenty-five as a lady-in-waiting to Teishi, the consort of the emperor Ichijō (986–1011), She wrote that one of the most splendid things in all the world was the Kagura sacred music performed in the foregarden of the Seiryōden. The following is her description of one such performance.

> It took place at night. On the white gravel spread in the foregarden, a temporary stage was erected; and, in each of its four corners fire burned in iron basketlike braziers, to illuminate the sacred dancing to take place there and to purify the stage for the descent of the god.* The first dance, called "Suruga," was a fantasy involving two dancers on the stage and depicting the descent from the sky of a celestial maiden in heavenly garments. The next told the story of the love and suffering of a mother searching for the child she had formerly abandoned. And last, as is customary at such performances, came the "Ōhire" finale. All the while, clappers, Korean flutes, flageolets, and harps were played, and songs were sung. Then, as the smoke from the garden flambeaux thinned, the sacred-dance flute shrilled in a wonderful and fascinating way.

Beyond the author's rapture in the beauty of this firelit scene, it is important to notice that on occasions of this kind, even if only temporarily, the gravel-spread areas became zones to which gods descended. Empty spaces spread with white gravel and consecrated to the gods were also created in the fifth and sixth centuries, before any histories of the garden were ever written.

At about this time the emperor became not just the head of a single clan, but ruler of the entire Japanese archipelago; in addition to his political duties, he was expected to act as priest to the gods. Thus the imperial palace, as the residence of a figure endowed with both sacred and secular power, had to be kept constantly purified and holy. The word *miya*, used in ancient times to mean both the residence of the emperor and a Shinto shrine, indicates the importance of ritual

---

*The music and dance here would be witnessed by the emperor before being dedicated to the gods. It was performed on three occasions: by unmarried female relations of the emperor about to leave the capital to serve as maidens at the Great Ise Shrine prior to the imperial coronation; as part of a festival held at the Iwashimizu Hachiman Shrine, in March; and as part of special festivals held for a day or two in November at the Kamo Shrine.

Sacred dance by torchlight in the Heian period. (From a Kamakura-period scroll.)

purity in the imperial home. Because it was a place not only where ministers assembled, but also where gods were worshiped, the court in front of the palace was spread with white sand as a symbol of this purity.

Changes in the functions of the emperor, however, led to a separation of garden functions as well. As time passed, the offices of sacred worship were relegated solely to Shinto priests, or *kannushi*; the emperor came to concern himself solely with political and military affairs. As this happened, the *miya* became a shrine pure and simple; the courtyard was converted into the rectangular space called *ishitsubo*, spread with fairly coarse, whitish-gray pebbles and found in all Shinto shrines to this day. The imperial residence became a state palace (*dairi*), but the front court spread with white gravel has persisted to the present.

Generating different kinds of meaning and content with the addition of stones, plants, ponds, streams, or tea-ceremony pavilions has converted the empty, sacred space of the ancient *niwa* into the Japanese garden in its various forms.

IDEALIZATION OF NATURE

To understand the Japanese garden, it is essential to understand the Japanese view of nature, since the two are deeply interrelated. In about the third century B.C., when the Japanese people settled in permanent villages to engage in rice cultivation, they inevitably created their first controlled, or secondary, environment in the form of agricultural land. In the early phase, when irrigation was still unsystematic, they had to rely on the forests; the springs and wetlands there lent themselves to paddy cultivation. The location of the Japanese islands in the monsoon belt provided the initial minimal conditions for such an agrarian culture, and though there were sometimes heavy rains, typhoons, blizzards, and floods, the climate was nonetheless considered a limitless blessing. The principle Shinto deity, the sun goddess Amaterasu, presides over abundant harvests; ethnologist Yanagida Kunio (1875–1962) observes that "farmers dug ponds on their own land and created streams to fill them because the sight and sound of flowing water calmed their

Tree with sacred Shinto rope. Ōmiwa Shrine, Nara.

minds [with the assurance of good crops]."

The Japanese thus cannot conceive of nature as hostile, an occasional threat to be propitiated; nor can they idealize nature as something perfect in itself. Around their houses, they created a secondary, controlled nature in the form of an open space or *niwa*. The *niwa* was an idealized version of nature: in addition to providing a place where some of the practical work of the farm could be done; it served as a "buffer zone" that protected the farm from high winds and snows and helped regulate humidity and temperature.

Natural phenomena were deified in primitive Japanese society. Though today practically no one believes literally in the power of nature gods, certain observances linger on as a matter of custom. Tree worship, which is said to persist in parts of Southeast Asia, is an interesting case in point. In Japan sacred, purifying ropes called *shimenawa* are still tied around the trunks of especially large, venerable trees, which are—in form at any rate—considered divine. Originally veneration of this kind no doubt sprang from a desire to understand the world and to propitiate the deities believed to govern it. It is easy to imagine that fear and adoration of the primeval forest also played a part in inspiring such reverence. Interestingly, the Japanese word for forest, *mori*, means both a stand of trees and a holy zone to which gods descend—in short, a shrine without a building. As long as the trees are there to serve as intermediaries with the god there is no need of architecture.

The initial step in the battle between man and gods can be interpreted as the felling of trees to expand agricultural land and to provide timber and firewood. To justify the cutting down of trees, the ancient Japanese used the timber first to construct a dwelling for the gods (*yashiro*), which they naturally took care to make finer than their own houses. As might be expected, these homes for the gods were closely associated with agriculture itself.

The Toro historical remains in Shizuoka Prefecture will illustrate the point. The Toro site is a primitive Japanese settlement of the Yayoi period (about 350 B.C. to A.D. 250), discovered in 1943 and since excavated and reconstructed. Here the inhabitants lived in pit dwellings that could be built with nothing more sophisticated than stone implements, but the storehouse is a much finer structure that would have required the use of iron ax, saw, and adze. Of course, the storehouse contained the precious seed rice without which no harvest could be expected the following year; this alone might account for the preeminence afforded it. But it must be remembered that, according to ancient belief, the spirit of the grain resided in the husk. The storehouse was, in short, more than a place where seed was kept: it was a shrine where the spirit of the grain resided. Probably for this reason, the main building of the Great Ise Shrine in Mie Prefecture, dedicated to the sun goddess and the main focus of Shinto worship for well over a thousand years, closely resembles the warehouses of the Yayoi period. Gradually the ancient storehouse became the nucleus of a purified zone (yuniwa) surrounded by the kind of gravel-spread region already described.

As farmers began to long for divine protection, in keeping with tree worship and as a sign of gratitude to the gods, they planted trees in the open space that surrounded their house. For this purpose, they selected old, drooping pines and cherries, whose pendant boughs were interpreted as proof that the gods would come down to earth.

In ancient Japanese society, both farmers and aristocrats alike wished to include in their garden spaces the same kinds of things: ponds, streams, and trees. They did not, however, use these elements on the same scale or in the same way. The common ground between their otherwise disparate approaches to the garden was the traditional aristocratic desire to re-create pastoral scenes in their homes. This desire inspired them to employ natural vistas, streams, country paths, and rural-style buildings, which they treated as objects of aesthetic appreciation. The longing on the part of the rich to reproduce in refined forms the rural environment of the poor is the source of the artificial hills and ponds that are an important part of all later Japanese landscaping.

Until the introduction of Western ideas in the nineteenth century, the Japanese gave little thought to the abstract beauty of nature. They chose to see the beautiful flower, not the beauty of the flower. Thus, from their standpoint, the important thing in gardening was the beauty of plants and stones that appear unaltered by human hands. They have never shown any interest in the appeal of flowers in geometrically plotted beds.

No natural ecological system, of course is static; gardens require human intervention if they are to remain as they were originally planned. Weeds and seedlings must be removed; trees and shrubbery must be pruned. In short, a garden becomes a kind of controlled tertiary environment because of the continuing care it demands. The meticulously controlled and groomed garden was originally most common in the Kyoto area; in contrast, some gardens in Tokyo and eastern Japan incorporated trees that, before the nineteenth century, were never found in Kyoto gardens—firs, zelkova, and so on—and let them grow naturally without pruning or trimming. Some of these trees flourished, and some withered. When they did, the gardeners never replaced them or tried to put the garden back in its original form, as the caretaker of a tightly controlled Kyoto-style garden would have done. This attitude assumes that trees, plants, and stones in nature are as much works of art as painting and sculpture, and attempts to make no distinctions between the natural and artificial.

This is not to imply, however, that the Japanese simply bring any old tree or boulder in from mountain or field and place it unaltered in their gardens. Just as the controlled garden demands that the shapes of plants be altered by pruning to suit aesthetic needs, stones must be carefully chosen for their shapes for each particular landscape. Though they tamper with materials, the Japanese strive to idealize nature in gardens that give the impression of naturalness; the workings of

Toro remains, Shizuoka.

Three-stone formation at Rakuraku-en, Shiga.

the human hand are found in all Japanese gardens, but the goals of artifice vary.

MICROCOSMS

The creation of a microcosm is a theme common to many aspects of Japanese culture: this is true of ikebana, bonsai, the tea ceremony, and gardening, to mention only a few. In a garden, stone arrangements constitute the spatial framework of this microcosm. Stones from mountains, fields, or seacoasts, whether completely untouched by human hands or hammered and chipped into fortuitously achieved shapes, are in themselves works of art of a kind, in one sense as valuable as what the artist fashions with his hands. But Japanese garden designers have not regarded stones as material through which to express their own ideas, as the stone-sculptor does; rather, they have selected from among naturally and fortuitously formed materials and have exerted their own ingenuity only in devising placements that produce the desired microcosmic effect. If there is an aesthetic element in this, it is the aesthetic of discovery.

The designers who long ago created the early prototypes of Japanese gardens did not work from such a clearly articulated philosophy. They simply saw and made use of things they thought were beautiful. The gardens were born of the happy concatenation of beautiful natural objects and people with minds receptive to that beauty. Questions of moral and aesthetic awareness must take precedence over gardening techniques and skills. In other words, a beautiful mind is essential to the creation of a beautiful garden.

To the Japanese mind, the dew drop glittering on a lotus leaf in the morning sun does not merely reflect, but concentrates and contains the sky and surrounding world on its shimmering surface. Similarly the whole garden, down to the flashing dewdrop, is not a thing isolated from the world but a condensation of all of nature. Three stones arranged in a garden stand for—and in a sense are—the classical Chinese triad of heaven, earth, and man.

A microcosm-garden needs a fence or hedge, not as a demarcation but as a connection between the world inside and the world outside. Japanese gardeners have always wanted to create the impression that the outside world is afloat within the garden space and to allow something of the garden to be, even if only fleetingly, visible from the outside. For instance, it has long been popular to let the

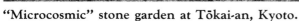

"Microcosmic" stone garden at Tōkai-an, Kyoto.   "Borrowed" landscape at Tenryū-ji, Kyoto.

boughs of an especially well-formed pine tree peep above a garden fence for the enjoyment of those outside. Perhaps an even more noteworthy gardening technique is the one called "borrowed scenery"—or, in gardener's terms, "scenery captured alive"—in which a distant view, or some part thereof, is incorporated into the garden space. There are a number of famous examples of this technique. The silhouette of distant Mount Hiei is an integral part of the gravel-and-stone (*kare sansui*) garden of the temple Entsū-ji in Kyoto. Mediating between the garden space and the mountain are a low hedge and a few trees, through the trunks of which we can see the beautiful scene. The mountain in the background, the foreground of the garden spaces, and the middle ground of hedge and trees combine to create one lovely picture.

At the Shugakuin Detached Palace, a spacious garden pond in the foreground contrasts with a distant view of the western and northern mountains. The element binding the composition together is the vast overspreading sky; this is an aesthetic consonant with the tradition of Oriental painting, in which empty spaces are as important as the spaces in which things are depicted. And just as there often appeared calligraphy and poetry in the empty spaces of the paintings, so in the spacious sky of the garden do there appear swollen banks of cloud, a descending sun at twilight, a passing rainstorm.

MUTABILITY AS A QUALITY OF PERMANENCY

The Buddhist doctrine that everything is ephemeral and that mutability is itself a cause of suffering has greatly influenced Japanese thinking. On the other hand, so has the idea that change itself is proof of life. From the Buddhist standpoint, the apparently permanent Pyramids of Egypt represent a desirable model; to see change as synonymous with life is to admire instead the flowing stream, never at rest and flecked with patches of foam that perpetually gather and disappear. In terms of garden design, where nature is the instructor, the Japanese have been under the influence of both ideas without being dominated exclusively by either.

(The ability to balance two ideas simultaneously in this way is characteristic of the Japanese people. From ancient times, a number of taboos have obtained in Japanese culture. For instance, since the written character for the number "four" is homophonous with that of the character for "death" and since ancient tradition

Heian courtiers enjoying the estate at Kōyō-in, Kyoto. (From a Kamakura-period scroll.)

assigns spirits to words, in Japan, though not in China, using four trees or four stones in a garden arrangement has been avoided. Any number of similar restrictions could be cited, but it would be a mistake to assert that the Japanese always abided by such taboos. It would be equally erroneous to say they invariably ignored them. The aim has always been to produce gardens that please, and the Japanese have become most adroit at finding ways to maintain the validity of taboos while actually violating them.)

Buddhism teaches that nothing has permanent identity; all things are made of constituent elements constantly in the process of change. In this connection the Japanese have tended to perceive in all phenomena a kind of universal mutability and interpermeability. An old folk song says that, by wearing a certain kind of hood, a person can hear the trees speak with human voices. Though perhaps in part derived from ancient tree worship, fundamentally this belief reflects the idea that gods can abide in trees, that they are friendly, and that they can be transmuted into human beings or even animals. All things are one; and none has an immutable identity.

The idea of change as a sign of life can be found in concrete terms in garden designs. For over a thousand years garden designers in Kyoto, long the center of the art, have employed only deciduous trees (with the single exception of the pine) because they present the richest visual variety—from the fresh green of spring, to full summer foliage, to the splendor of autumn leaves, and then to the beauty of snow on bare winter branches. The diary *Goshō nikki* mentioned above describes the pleasure that court aristocrats of the Heian period took in the changing of the seasons:

> The master of the house and his guests together enjoyed observing the ponds and streams that had been created in the residence garden. Nor was their enjoyment limited to the flowers of spring and the brilliantly colored foliage of autumn. In summer, they could escape the heat in the cool breezes that blew through the fishing pavilion overlooking the pond. And in winter they could forget the cold by reading poetry as they gazed at the snowclad garden in the morning. Delighting in such scenery, the master of the house felt blessed enough to live for a hundred years.

Veranda, sliding doors, and open interior of a traditional Japanese house in Takayama, Gifu.

Things that change are incomplete. They have nothing of the absolute in them and can never achieve ideal forms. The tree that flourishes now must someday wither and die. The changing of the seasons is only a process, and the garden partakes of blessedness and eternity because it is always incomplete. People who gently observe this mutability and realize that they too are a changing part of changing nature find peace of mind. Embracing this view, it has never occurred to the Japanese to create gardens that oppose or contrast with nature. Indeed, they have always preferred to feel as if they lived entirely in the natural world, to which they have to a large extent opened their residential spaces. It is true that in the West today many houses have large picture windows that make nature seem close. But the glass in the windows is usually permanently fixed in place, and the only contact between the people inside and the world of nature outside is visual. The traditional Japanese house is very different, connecting to the garden through spacious openings created by freely sliding panels (*shōji*) that provide ready egress to the outside. Furthermore, to create a protective space around the interior core while making possible a comfortable appreciation of nature, the traditional house is usually built with a veranda. In that it is roofed and on the same level as the rooms beyond it, the veranda is part of the interior; in that it can be totally opened on one side (sometimes more) and is in direct contact with the outside air, it partakes of the exterior as well. No doubt the veranda is based on the needs of an agricultural people dwelling in the monsoon zone and not on knowledge of natural ecology.

The Japanese sensitivity to change extends even to the alterations worked by the passage of time—albeit very, very slowly—in stones. The patina (*sabi*) produced in their natural environments—whether it be beach, field, or mountain—accounts for much of the beauty of stones and dictates how they will be selected for particular landscaping needs. Even after they are set in the garden, moreover, stones continue to collect a new kind of patina (called garden *sabi*), which is largely the responsibility of the person who cares for them.

This chapter looks at the forms of the Japanese garden and how they evolved, from the early hill-and-pond gardens of Heian times to the spacious and elaborate landscapes for strolling and recreation built from about the seventeenth century. In all these gardens, the basic building blocks were the same: combinations of stones, water, and plants.

STONES, WATER, PLANTS

Ryōgen-in. Good placement of a stone artfully blends the irregular shape and weathered aspect of the natural material with the human designer's more formal principles of balance and aesthetic beauty. The tall, vertical stone flanked by lower horizontal shapes is a standard treatment. Here, the tilt of the main stone gives the arrangement enormous tension. (Kyoto)

Daisen-in. Stones of various textures suggest a bridge over a torrent at the point where it emerges from a mountain chasm. This design is based on Chinese landscape paintings, and it exemplifies the Zen belief that even the smallest space can contain a microcosm of the vast universe. The sensitivity to stone that made this garden possible, however, derives in no small measure from Japan's animist Shinto tradition. (Kyoto)

Saihō-ji Upper Garden. This stone "cascade" is one of the earliest (ca. 1340) examples of dry-landscape techniques and one of the greatest achievements of Japanese garden art. The viewer at its base is nearly overwhelmed by the aggressive verticality of the overall design, but this is expertly modulated by the stable horizontal stones and the mossy pools between the stages. Rust on the stones and the slightly overgrown surroundings add to the almost palpable timelessness of the site. (Kyoto)

Jōei-ji. This garden is said to have been designed by Sesshū (1420-1506), a great landscape painter admired for his chunky, bold style. There is something of that same look about the flat-topped rocks here, but the impression is of a vast open universe rather than a particular panorama. Azalea clumps echo the stones and help unify the composition. (Yamaguchi)

Ryōgen-in. A courtyard garden—*tsuboniwa*—can open up the inner space of a structure or, as here, help to connect two buildings. It is also a light trap, a function enhanced in this garden by the white, reflective gravel bed. The two complementary stone groupings tie the ends of the long corridor together in a highly abstract Zen composition. (Kyoto)

Kohō-an. A flat stone along a pathway suggests a bridge over a river. This is part of a larger garden that depicts famous landscape scenes of China and is meant to be viewed from an adjacent tea room as if seated in a boat at anchor. A reconstruction from the 1790s, it is considered faithful to the original design of Kobori Enshū (1579-1647), one of the great garden builders of the time. (Kyoto)

Ichijōdani Asakura Residence. For a hundred years until the mid-1500s, the Asakura lords ruled from their castle in the narrow gorge of Ichijōdani in Echizen province. In the 1960s, this garden was unearthed there, revealing a pond, craggy island, and dry cascade. The composition strikes some modern observers as untidy, but the many massive boulders are interesting and appropriate to a warrior's estate. (Fukui)

Sentō Palace. This vast garden, with its two ponds, paths for strolling, large wisteria trellis, and tea houses, was originally designed by Kobori Enshū in the 1630s as a residence for the retired emperor Gomizuno-o and his wife. Each of the cobblestones forming the famous beach of the southern pond was brought in from Odawara, far to the east. The smooth sweep of the coastline here forms a pleasant contrast to the more rugged stonework on the opposite shore. (Kyoto)

Hekiun-sō. Flat stones form a beach landing and effectively lead the eye across the surface of a pond to a pavilion, boathouse, and forest. A path borders this pond and presents ever-changing vistas in traditional stroll-garden style. Before 1917, when financier Nomura Tokushichi began to develop the site, there was nothing here but rice paddies. (Kyoto)

Tenryū-ji. This garden was designed in about 1340 by Musō Soseki, who also built the Saihō-ji. The rockwork in this section of the shoreline is decidedly manmade. The bridge, in three segments, serves as a walkway, as a part of the design, and as a metaphor: it represents the three faiths of Buddhism, Confucianism, and Taoism that must be mastered and then transcended to reach enlightenment. (Kyoto)

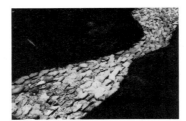

Shinnyo-in. Built in 1569, this garden was restored after the war by Shigemori Mirei. Large cobblestones all with the same downstream orientation produce a vigorous dry-landscape that evokes not only the speed and energy of a torrent, but its crashing sound. Bringing the moss all the way down gives the impression of swollen banks. It's hard to imagine this as a scene for restful contemplation. (Kyoto)

Hekiun-sō. Water becomes an elaborate musical and rhythmic instrument in the garden. Designers particularly favor shallow bottoms in their streams, because this makes the water run faster and creates more opportunities for sound and visual effects.

Hōkongō-in. The waterfall, while it provides a pleasing sound and appearance, is also a device for bringing in water without exposing pipes or earthworks. The one shown here, built ca. 1130, is among the oldest in Japan and is all that remains of a larger garden that comprised a pond, an Amida hall, and other structures. It is made of five hefty, magnificent stones and stands 4 meters tall. (Kyoto)

Tōfuku-ji. Square granite slabs in a sea of moss suggest paddy fields but are here a formal design element. This garden was built by Shigemori Mirei in 1939 and appeals to modern tastes without representing a complete break from the past. The spacing between the stones is deliberately irregular and, at the border of the plot where there are larger plantings, thins out as a means of linking the two zones. (Kyoto)

Daichi-ji. Plants in traditional gardens are usually pruned and shaped, either to "reveal" their natural form or, as here, to suggest mountains, the sea, or boulders. This hedge, said to have been designed by Kobori Enshū's grandson, is a huge representation of the sea with a treasure ship being tossed among the waves. The full curves, highlighted by shadows, resemble the scrolling patterns that appear on much of the decorative art of the period. (Shiga)

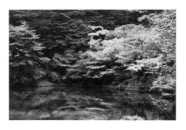

Shugakuin Detached Palace. Upper Villa. Shugakuin was a country retreat built by the retired emperor Gomizuno-o in the seventeenth century. It is a garden on a grand scale, covering three levels, with numerous buildings and an expansive sense of the great outdoors. Few things are more beautiful than Shugakuin's autumn foliage, especially here, at Maple Valley, in a corner of the Pond of the Bathing Dragon. (Kyoto)

Ōmori Residence. Low basins made of stone (*tsukubai*) hold water that can be used to wash before the tea ceremony, to sprinkle on the stones and plants, or to create a stream. The stone lantern is a vertical prop that traditionally provided illumination around the basin at night. The courtyard garden here is very small; in most cases a gardener would use elements sparingly to open up the space, but this garden swells with material and is very inviting. (Kyoto)

Hōkoku-ji. Hōkoku-ji is popularly called the Bamboo Temple, and this little forest behind the main hall is the reason why. The diffuse light and lack of undergrowth suggest the atmosphere of a cedar forest on a mountain slope, but this place is only a short walk from a crowded shopping area. The trouble with bamboo is that it spreads rapidly—used heedlessly it will quickly turn any open plot into a forest. Not a favorite plant in the Japanese garden. (Kamakura)

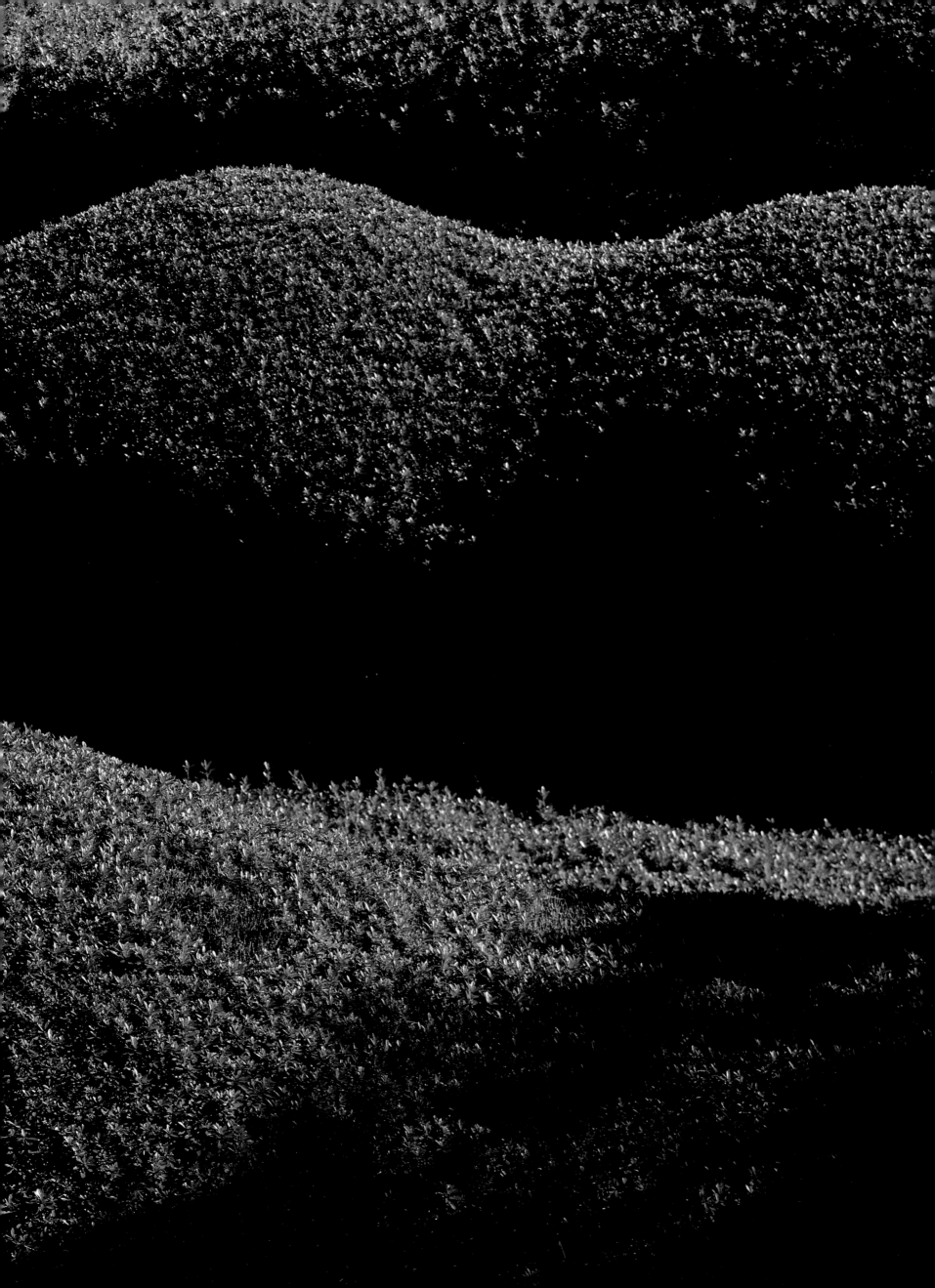

A HISTORY OF
THE JAPANESE GARDEN

The Japanese *niwa* (a word conveniently but not entirely accurately translated as "garden") originated from two main sources: religion and agriculture. Religion—and by extension government, which was initially conceived of in terms of religious ceremony—brought into being the sanctified open space spread with gravel, typified today by the foregarden of the Kyoto Imperial Palace and the courtyards of Shinto shrines. Farming made demands for outdoor spaces, where chores could be done when weather permitted, and for indoor spaces where some of those same tasks could still be performed when weather was inclement. The front yard (*niwa*) and the earth-floored interior anteroom (*doma*) or side-passage garden of the farmhouse were designed to meet those needs; in its root forms, the word *niwa* means not so much a stretch of ground as a place (*ha*) for a specific purpose where artificially treated, fine-grain clay (*ni*) is used.

Though fundamentally functional, the *doma* and the front yard were not without ceremonial and religious significance. The *doma*, for example, where the cooking took place, was decorated at the New Year with special cakes of pounded glutinous rice called *kagami-mochi* in honor of the gods of fire and water. Primarily a place for drying rice bran in the sun, the front yard was where etiquette dictated that the head of the house conduct his guests for ceremonious leave-takings; the custom still persists in some rural regions.

As farm work zones, *niwa* continued to play a major part in agricultural life until fairly recently, although the original forms of the front yard and the *doma* are often missing in farmhouses constructed after World War II. It was not such homely spaces, however, but the gravel-spread empty expanse serving the needs of emperor and aristocrats that inspired what the world now knows as the art of Japanese landscaping. Early forms were beginning to emerge in the late fifth and early sixth centuries; by this time, a government centered on the imperial house and court and located in the Yamato basin had assumed

Earth-floored interior of an 18th-century home.

Modern stone garden by Nagare Masayuki. Tenrikyō Building, Tokyo.

control of most of the archipelago. This government was vigorously striving to elevate the level of national culture by importing Chinese and Korean ideas, among them the religio-philosophical systems of Taoism, Confucianism, and Buddhism—which later came to influence garden philosophy, forms, and techniques.

Importations have played a formative role in the evolution of most aspects of Japanese culture. It is important to remember, however, that such borrowing never entails the notion of abandoning the related or corresponding indigenous elements. The introduction of Chinese garden plans and forms, for example, did not spell the end of older Japanese plans and forms: the two were allowed to coexist side by side. This approach has prevailed throughout the ages; the white-gravel foregarden of the Kyoto Imperial Palace is Heian period (794–1185) in style, though constructed in the mid-nineteenth century; it symbolizes the way in which traditional values have held their own over the ages, afforded importance on a par with the latest novelties.

It should be reiterated that when ideas about gardens were borrowed, virtually no one correctly understood what they were borrowing. Misinterpretations—whether of ignorance or accident—combined with native Japanese garden ideas to generate still different forms. It may be true, as some people claim, that merely adopting without comprehending betokens an utter lack of independent thought. Ironically, however, by making no attempt to understand the philosophy behind the borrowed garden styles, and superficially distorting or misinterpreting them, the Japanese have been able to assimilate what was foreign while protecting the independence of what was their own.

In period after historical period, new and different forms have emerged: the garden with artificial hill and pond of the Nara and Heian periods (646–1185), the dry stone-and-gravel garden of the Muromachi period (1333–1568), and the spacious gardens for strolling planned for princes and feudal lords in the Edo period (1615–1868) are cases in

point. But in no instance were old forms and styles cast aside to make room for the new. Old and new—at a later date, Eastern and Western—have shared places in Japan, coeval and appreciated in all periods, rather than piled on one another in strata like the levels of an archaeological excavation. In the history of Japanese gardening, the ancient and the novel, the Oriental and the Occidental, stand like books on a shelf, to be consulted and used—or misinterpreted—at any time.

ISLES OF ETERNAL BLISS

An early form of the aristocratic Japanese garden featured a prominent pond, almost always graced with islands, symbolizing the sea and the Everlasting Land, or Tokoyo, and the Three Islands of the Blessed: Hōrai, Hōjō, and Eishū.

During the Ice Age, some of the distant forebears of the Japanese may have walked from the Asian continent over a land bridge that has long since vanished. It is virtually certain that others arrived after the Ice Age in small boats, on the warm currents from the south. If the sea has isolated Japan, it has also been the road over which dauntless people have flaunted danger to reach the archipelago. And from time immemorial, the Japanese people, now a homogeneous racial amalgam of all these far wanderers, have believed that somewhere over the waters is the mystical land of Tokoyo.

When this legend first came into being is a mystery. The annals known as the *Nihon shoki* (compiled in 720) contain a story of a dwarf named Sukunahikona-no-kami, who with the god Ōkuninushi-no-mikoto created the sub-celestial world; he is credited with the invention of hot-springs baths, medicine, and the art of brewing saké. In one version of the myth, Sukunahikona-no-kami climbed a millet stalk from which he was transported to the Everlasting Land. In the ancient tale of Mizue no Urako (better known as Urashima Tarō) the hero is saved from drowning by a sea turtle who takes him to the land of

Design of Blessed Island on vase given to Tōdai-ji, Nara, in 767.

Tortoise (top) and crane "islands" at Funda-in, Kyoto.

Tokoyo. There are various interpretations of the derivation of its name, but Tokoyo has always been thought of as a very distant place out in the sea, removed from the realm of actuality and, though mysterious in many respects, free of neither unhappiness nor death.

The influence of Taoism, introduced from China in about the sixth century, altered the old vision to convert Tokoyo into something like the Chinese ideal land of the sages, where people never grow old or die. It too was still believed to exist far out over the sea. The bird of this mystical land was the crane, considered to be a messenger of the gods. On the Islands of the Blessed, Hōrai, Hōjō, and Eishū, grew trees whose fruit prolonged life. The very insects there had wonderful spiritual powers. This was the realm where dwelt immortal sages possessed of great supernatural gifts.

The Japanese aristocrats lived in the Nara region, however, cut off by the surrounding mountains from any view of the sea. In their desire to establish some kind of contact with the Everlasting Land they believed to lie over the waves, and to compensate for their isolation from the sea, they created gardens for their mansions that included ponds and artificial islands.

The open area spread with gravel remained indispensable for ceremonial purposes, and even with the introduction of these new symbolic versions of paradise over the sea, the ceremonial ground was left intact: the pond was dug beyond it. In the pond were symbolic, artificial islands (shima), the inclusion of which led to the use of the word shima as a generic name for such gardens. The pond was fed by a stream that in theory had to flow from east to west; in fact, misinterpretations allowed the Japanese to justify practically any direction of flow.

The Nihon shoki and the eighth-century poetry anthology called Man'yōshū contain descriptions of one such pond-and-island arrangement on the grounds of the mansion of Soga no Umako (–626?) at Shima-no-shō, in the village of Asuka in what is now Nara Prefecture. Soga

no Umako was an astonishing man of great influence. Through his relations with the imperial house and his advocacy of Buddhism, at the time a new and controversial import from China, he overcame his political rivals the Mononobe clan and was even able to have the emperor Sushun (–592?) assassinated. He himself had helped put Sushun on the throne but later came to entertain grave doubts about him. Umako also founded the Hōkō-ji, the first Buddhist temple ever erected in Japan.

Though farmlands today obscure all traces, presumably a man of his position and influence was able to build a very splendid home for himself. The entry for the year 626 in the Nihon shoki describes the garden of his mansion and refers to Umako as the "Minister of the Islands"; a poem in the Man'yōshū makes mention of Umako's pond, where he kept brightly colored mandarin ducks and where the white blossoms of the plant Pieris japonica could be seen in the spring.

After the Soga met their downfall, Umako's mansion served as a residence, first for the emperor Tenmu (–686) and then for the prince Kusakabe (662–89). In 682, a red tortoise was presented to the prince and set loose in the pond. The tortoise—like the crane—is considered a symbol of longevity, and since a red one was especially unusual, it was hoped the gift would portend good fortune and long life for the prince. In fact he died of an illness in his late twenties. Some of his guards composed the more than twenty elegiac verses to his memory included in the Man'yōshū anthology, among them these two:

Around the island boulders, now that you are gone, grows grass that was not there when you were here.

Will we see again the azalea-flooded path by the boulder-bordered flowing of the pond?

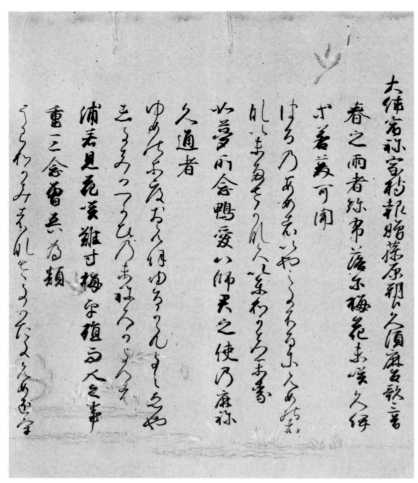

Northwest coast of Shikoku, near the Inland Sea.

PROTOTYPE COMPLETED

The verses quoted above imply two things about the prince's garden. First, they suggest that its central feature was indeed the pond-and-island arrangement blending the indigenous belief in the Everlasting Land (Tokoyo) and imported Chinese ideas about the realm of the immortal sages. Second, the mention of boulders, grasses, and azaleas implies that such garden scenes were idealized versions of vistas one could enjoy by visiting the seashore, the fields, and the mountains.

In addition to giving earthly form to their hopes for eternal happiness, aristocratic homeowners were inspired to reproduce in their gardens the beautiful scenes they all observed during the boat and horseback journeys to outlying posts where they served as provincial governors or envoys. The first great panorama most of them would encounter was almost certainly the calm waters and numerous islands of the Seto Inland Sea: over 400 kilometers long, this was the water route over which all voyagers to western Japan—and beyond to Korea and China—had to travel. The pleasant recollections of such scenery, and the belief in Tokoyo and other legends of eternal felicity, doubtless played a part in determining the designs of the gardens they created for themselves at home again in the capital city.

The case of a certain Ōtomo no Tabito (665–731) suggests what must have been the mental state of those who returned to the imperial court with memories of their experiences of happiness and grief in distant places. Ōtomo was in charge of the *dazaifu*, the government's special branch for foreign affairs on the island of Kyushu. In 730 he returned to Nara, having been appointed to the rank of great councilor (*dainagon*). He arrived there in September, when the year begins to grow old. Thirty-five at the time, he had lost his beloved wife, Ōtomo no Iratsume, two years earlier and lived in loneliness. I cannot help believing that the image of the Inland Sea overlapped in his mind's eye with much else he had seen, as he looked at the

garden he created in Nara with his wife's help, in happier times, and composed this verse: "Now the trees grow tall, beloved, in the garden [*shima*] we made then."

In the latter part of the Nara period, as the older system of land allotment failed, great manors passed into the possession of temples, shrines, and aristocratic families. Naturally, the owners of these estates had to visit their holdings from time to time and ensure that they were managed properly. Since these manors were spread out all over the country, the journeys brought to aristocratic eyes many lovely natural scenes besides those of the Seto Inland Sea. Impressions of this scenery influenced garden design back in the capital city. In the garden of his mansion at Kawara-in, for example, the Minister of the Left, Minamoto no Tōru (822–95), re-created something like the beautiful vista of pineclad islands at a place called Shiogama, 640 kilometers to the north in the province of Mutsu. In about 1035, Ōnakatomi no Sukechika at his Rokujō-in residence created a version of the famous wooded sand spit called Ama no Hashidate, at Tango on the Japan Sea coast, which even today is rated as one of Japan's three great natural panoramas.

In both these instances, as in the gardens mentioned in Tachibana no Toshitsuna's eleventh-century work on landscaping, *Sakutei-ki*, the pond is still intended to represent the sea. But it is important to note the subtle alteration in attitude that had already taken place by this time. In the earlier period, religious or semi-religious considerations always dictated the use of ponds and islands as the central features of aristocratic gardens. In a somewhat later period, however, though the religious element persists, ponds, islands, and plantings tend to be included as much to evoke famous natural scenes, especially those mentioned in classical literature, as to symbolize aspirations for eternal life and bliss.

Increasingly crowded urban conditions, too, played a part in shaping the period's tastes in garden design. For a while after Heian-kyō (modern Kyoto) became the capital in 794,

Ama no Hashidate.

Rendering of Ama no Hashidate at Katsura Detached Palace, Kyoto.

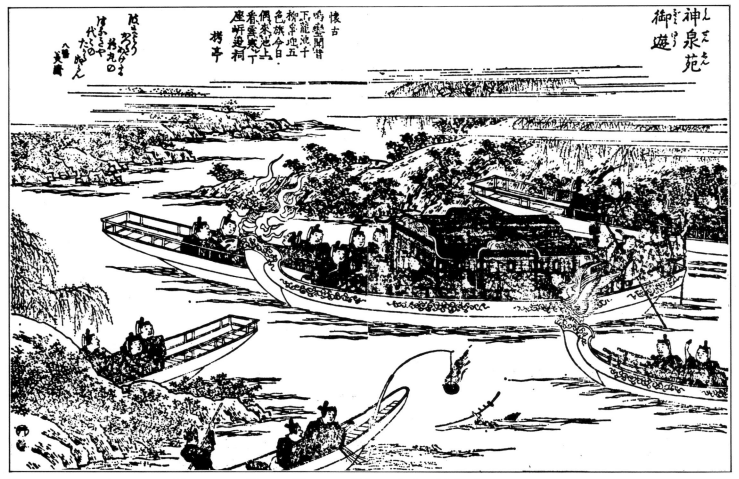

Heian courtiers boating at Shinsen-en, Kyoto. (From an Edo-period guidebook.)

hunting was still possible in the compounds and parks of aristocratic estates. As the urban population grew denser, however, more and more houses and other buildings went up, diminishing these expanses of pristine woodland. Before long, the emperor and his courtiers found themselves forced to make excursions to the suburbs when they wanted a little room to breathe. In those days, the suburban setting was still almost entirely undisturbed. What farmhouses existed were few and far between. Sparkling streams flowed through open fields where lovely flowers bloomed; on hills and mountains grew great stands of red pine and deciduous trees. Back in their stately city homes, surrounded by massive tile-coped, plaster-finished clay walls, aristocrats who longed to recapture the beauty they found outside the city used ordinary trees, grasses, stones, and streams—nature's own works of art—in the making of strictly nongeometric idealizations of natural scenery.

Gardens of this kind ultimately blended with the white-gravel gardens descended from ceremonial foregardens and shrine courtyards to produce the prototypical Japanese garden, or *teien* (*tei* representing the open courtyard spread with gravel, and *en* the planted garden)—from which all later developments in the Japanese garden evolved.

ASSIMILATING ALIEN GODS

The two dates usually given for the introduction of Buddhism into Japan from the Asian mainland are A.D. 538 and 552. It is almost certain, however, that Korean immigrants practiced the Buddhist faith in Japan before either of those dates, though no doubt only among themselves and without impressive temple compounds. In the sixth century, in the reign of the emperor Kinmei (510–70), when Japan lost the last of the bases it had formerly held on the Korean peninsula, the religion was officially admitted. While it became a bone of great contention between the Soga and the Mononobe families, early Buddhist thought exerted no

influence on Japanese garden design.

The Japanese initially looked to Buddhism for a variety of other benefits. Without a writing system of their own, they were eager to learn the Chinese characters in which the Buddhist scriptures they imported were recorded. Further, they were fascinated by gilded Buddhist sculpture, delicately wrought ritual furnishings, and splendid vermilion-painted temple buildings—an architectual style never seen in Japan before. They seem to have thought of the Buddha himself as no more than another of the myriad deities they had grown accustomed to in their own native religion, though he was of course an alien god. In effect they attempted to assimilate Buddhism while leaving their own pantheon of gods infact.

The first true Buddhist temple in Japan was the Hōkō-ji, the tutelary temple of the Soga family, built with Korean technical guidance between 585 and 609. (The Hōryū-ji, the oldest extant Buddhist temple in Japan, was built for Prince Shōtoku in 607 but later burned. The oldest of the present buildings was rebuilt in 670.)

In 645, when the power of the old ruling clans was finally overcome and the government established a bureaucratic system based on Chinese models, it turned eagerly to Buddhist philosophy as a means of unifying the nation. In contrast to Shinto, which in its primitive form had no doctrines or formal teachings, Buddhism arrived with a complete philosophical system transcending differences of clan and region; it was made to order for a government eager to consolidate its control. It was no longer the clan or the family, but the Buddha who gave the individual human being meaning and value. The Buddha's blessings determined one's happiness in life; prayers to the Buddha ensured the peace and well-being of the dead.

By allying itself with this transcendent authority, the government intended to assert its superiority to all other social and political institutions in Japan. To make this relation clear to all, the emperor commissioned the

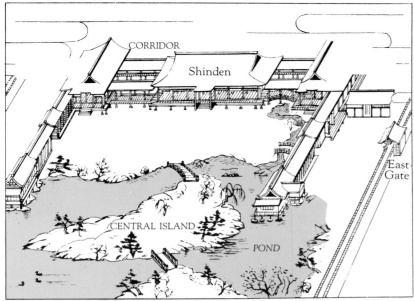

Typical Heian architecture, so-called "shinden" style, with pavilions, bridge, pond, island, and decorative plantings.

Yume-tagae Kannon, a Buddhist image belonging to Horyū-ji, Kyoto. Ca. 7th century.

building of a number of temples; the first of these was the Kudara-tai-ji, the construction of which began in 639. In 677 the first of the so-called official temples, the Taikan-tai-ji (later called the Daian-ji) was completed.

The series of imperial- and government-sponsored temple projects reached its zenith with the construction in Nara (then the capital) of the Tōdai-ji, whose main hall (Daibutsu-den) is still the largest wooden structure in the world. Construction began in 749. Because of its importance as a physical symbol of the unity of the nation under Buddhism—and by association under the imperial house—the Tōdai-ji was intended to be large and splendid in every respect. In addition to its immense main hall, it had numerous large and imposing buildings; great lengths of roofed corridors; and a pair of seven-level pagodas 100 meters tall, each in its own compound.

Even in this splendor and glory, Buddhism still had no effect on gardening as such. The temples were surrounded with walls. The courtyards had only gravel surfaces. The gates were rarely opened, nor were ordinary people free to enter them at will. The government's major interest was that the magnificent temple halls and towers should soar above surrounding buildings and forests to symbolize the blessings of the Buddha and the people's subjugation to the established political order.

In 794 the capital was moved from the Nara basin to Heian-kyō (modern Kyoto). In the ninth century, new developments took place in Japanese Buddhism and in the kinds of temples it required. Two great Japanese priests visited China to study in the early part of the ninth century and brought back with them the teachings they encountered there: Kūkai (774–835) with the *mantra* teachings upon which he founded the Shingon sect, and Saichō (767–822) with the Tiantai teachings which became the basis for Japanese Tendai Buddhism.

Shingon belongs in the category of what is called "esoteric" Buddhism, in which enlightenment depends on rituals imparted only to the priesthood. Tendai Buddhism,

The Daibutsu-den at Tōdai-ji, Nara.

Aerial view of Enryaku-ji atop Mount Hiei, Kyoto.

too, gradually absorbed more and more secret elements until it became an esoteric sect. The basic approach is emotional: believers achieve the desired state of mind as they sit in halls dimly lit by flickering oil lamps, listening to priests who chant sutras before a ritual fire (*goma*) that is believed to purge evil. The Shingon sect, furthermore, has an extensive pantheon of deities; this would seem to run counter to the basic teachings of Buddhism, which insist that human beings must look to themselves for salvation and rely on no outside assistance. In its earliest stages of development, however, esoteric Buddhism encountered many forms of indigenous worship as it spread from country to country. It neither rejected nor subjected itself to these alien gods, but chose instead to incorporate and assimilate; this is what happened when esoteric Buddhism encountered the deities of Shinto.

As part of its strict discipline, esoteric Buddhism preferred to build monasteries on mountaintops where the climate was severe. In 785, Saichō decided to build his main temple, now called Enryaku-ji, on Mount Hiei, not far from Kyoto. To avoid offending the resident gods, a compromise was made whereby the Buddhist temple was placed on the pinnacle and the Shinto Hie Shrine on the lower reaches; this approach ultimately found theoretical justification in the doctrine that the Shinto gods were actually reincarnations of Buddhas and bodhisattvas. In a very real sense, Shinto and Buddhism united.

Esoteric temples were free of the roofed corridors and enclosing walls that had characterized Buddhist temples of other sects. Their compounds were the sacred forests in which they stood. In other words, the temple compound had come to partake very much of the nature of the *niwa* of the Shinto shrine. This at last created a set of circumstances in which Buddhist thought was able—two centuries after its introduction into Japan—to influence Japanese gardening.

On the grounds of the Shinto Achi Shrine in the city of Kurashiki west of Osaka, for example, is a huge granite

The priest Kūkai, also called Kōbō Daishi.

Sacred boulder at Miwayama, Nara.

boulder revered as a deity; garden historian Shigemori Mirei considers this kind of stone to be the source from which all later Japanese landscape stone arrangements evolved. Characteristic of the fusion of Shinto and Buddhism, the Achi Shrine was traditionally administered by the neighboring Buddhist temple Kanryū-ji. As this fusion continued, the Shinto *niwa* became part of a system of gardening philosophy.

PARADISES ON EARTH

The culture of the Heian period (794–1185) was dominated by the court and aristocracy of Kyoto, with its all-consuming aesthetic sensibilities. The aristocrats were largely responsible for the prospering of esoteric Buddhism, which, though equipped with a full battery of doctrines and teachings, relied heavily for its emotional appeal upon beautiful colors, patterns, and forms in its ceremonies. It was the aristocrats who created from the general background of esoteric Buddhism a belief that the Buddha would save all those who earnestly beseech him from the six karma-determined evil ways of hell, ravenous demons, beasts, demons of wrath, humanity, and heaven and transport them to his paradise of Sukhavati located in the west. The Tendai priest Genshin (942–1017), who strongly influenced the art associated with belief in Sukhavati, taught that one could break the bonds of attachment to the phenomenal world through an understanding of three truths: that all things are insubstantial, that all things nonetheless have provisional reality, and that the Middle Way transcends both substantiality and insubstantiality. Achieving this understanding was tantamount to immediate attainment of paradise; hence the philosophical position that paradise could be created on earth.

This came as a great relief to the imperial house, the court aristocracy, and the aristocratic warrior class. The old social structure was crumbling before their eyes; the nation was plagued with war, famine, and natural disaster. In their longing for security and happiness, the affluent

Taima mandala, ca. 9th century. (From a Kamakura-period copy.)

attempted to create their own paradises on earth in the form of temples to the Buddha Amida.

Mandalas provided images of paradise for the imagination to work with, but mandalas were no more than phantom representations. Paradises on earth had to be expressed in real gardens and buildings, the beauty of the whole composition centered on a hall that contained a gilded statue of the Buddha Amida and faced a pond. Lit by myriad lanterns that drove back the dark, the statue cast a glittering reflection on the water. Flowers and fragrant incense were arrayed before it. The voices of priests chanting the sutras echoed through the hall; the ceiling and posts were decorated with gold, silver, and mother-of-pearl. The carved figures of celestial musicians seemed to drift dancing downward from on high.

In a work called the *Eiga monogatari* (eleventh century) there is the following description of the paradise the regent Fujiwara no Michinaga (966–1027) built for himself at the magnificent temple Hōjō-ji in 1022.

The stones of the garden gleamed like water sprites. Lotuses floated on the ripples of the clear and limpid pond; in the water the statue of the Buddha Amida in the main hall, the other halls, sutra libraries, and bell towers reflected in all directions. The place seemed to be truly the world of the Buddha. The leaves of the garden trees rustled, though no wind blew. Their leaves were the blue of lapis lazuli. A bridge spanned the pond of Seven Precious Substances. From the bottom of the pond could be seen the graceful branches of jewel trees. On the beach of a small island in the pond played peacocks and parrots.

The site of the temple was over 200 meters square. The most important of the various buildings on it was the Amida hall, 11 bays wide by 5 bays deep. The inner part of the hall, with its 5-meter statue of Amida, was painted with gold lacquer and lavishly decorated with mother-of

Byōdō-in Phoenix Hall at night.

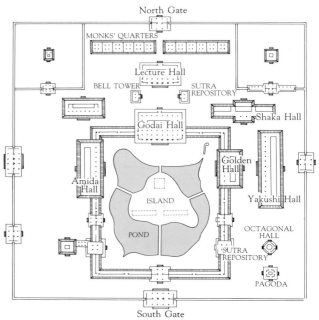

Plan of Hōjō-ji and paradise garden, ca. 1020.

pearl and gems. In the outer part of the hall Michinaga himself meditated, prayed, and read the sutras. With the principal image stood nine other statues of Amida; from their hands hung silken cords in variegated colors, drawn together in the hands of the main figure and extending to the meditation room—where, in this aura of paradisiacal splendor, the cords leading from Amida clenched in his own hands, Michinaga died in 1027.

Beautiful Amida halls like this one were invariably set in gardens of equal splendor and loveliness. It is interesting to give some thought to the way such expensive projects were financed, and to the people who planned and executed them. The funds for buildings and gardens alike came from the aristocrats themselves and from provincial governors. Michinaga was responsible for appointing people to these governorships; anyone who wanted an appointment would build a hall or other temple building or undertake a gardening project for Michinaga in return.

The gardens were designed and built by low-ranking

Buddhist priests of the esoteric sects, called *ishitatesō*, or "stone-setting priests." Some of their names and the gardens on which they worked are known. Most of them were assigned to the temple Ninna-ji, at the time one of the most prestigious Tendai temples. As evidence of its close association with gardening, it is known that the residential subtemple Shinren-in of the Ninna-ji possessed a scroll text on garden design and construction called *Illustrations of Landscapes and Fields (Senzui narabini yagyō no zu)*.

In the period under discussion, the making of gardens was entrusted to priests because the work required knowledge of Buddhist philosophy and rules. Those priests were of low rank because, until at least the end of the sixteenth century, all labor involving work with soil—well digging, kiln construction, wall plastering, road grading, and so on—was considered debasing, to be performed only by people of low social standing. Gardener priests may have come particularly from the Ninna-ji because the

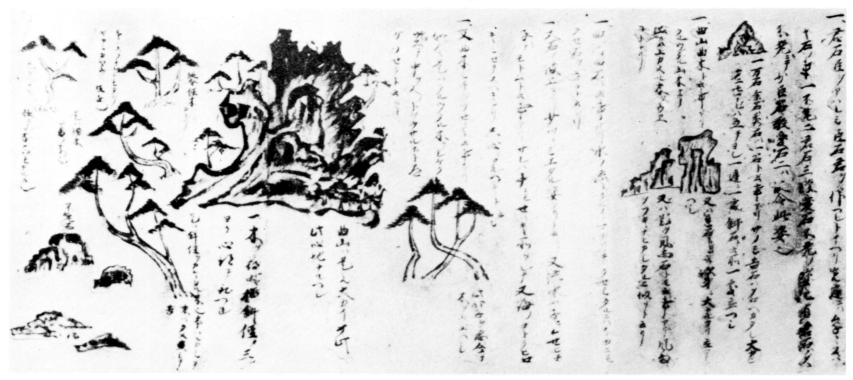

Section of "Senzui narabini yagyō no zu" dealing with shapes of plants and stones.

temple had close connections with the imperial family as well as numerous subtemples of its own, affording abundant opportunity for landscaping work; it may also have been simply that the right kinds of stones and trees were in ample supply nearby.

Buddhism in any case brought to flower a kind of garden in the "re-created paradise" style that was to persist from the end of the twelfth to the beginning of the fourteenth century. This was the first of the heavily Buddhist-influenced Japanese garden styles. And when it died out it was not because either esoteric Buddhism or faith in the paradise of the Buddha Amida had failed: it died because the warrior class, which had seized political power from the court aristocrats, preferred the strict precepts and disciplines of Zen Buddhism, and the gardens it created—plain arrangements of stone and gravel symbolizing the entire universe.

THE SHOGUN AND THE OUTCAST

The year 1428 brought famine and plague. It also brought the first peasant uprising in Japanese history, against the Ashikaga shogunate. The uprising began when peasants from Ōmi province (modern Shiga) presented the government with the demand for a moratorium on the debts they had incurred with pawnbrokers. It was a difficult time for the shogunate in other respects. The imperial house had split into two rival courts, one in Kyoto and one on Mount Yoshino, south of Nara. Ultimately the Kyoto court prevailed, but straggling adherents of the Yoshino court and other warriors who opposed the shogunate raided the capital city, causing great damage and suffering. In the end, the emperor, though politically impotent, retained his symbolic prestige; the shogunal government, though shaken, stood firm.

The warriors were the ruling class, and they gave generous support to the temples of Zen Buddhism. These temples grew in size and influence, serving the warrior class as guides to moral and cultural values.

In that same year of 1428, in a work entitled *Kennaiki*, a certain Madenokōji Tokifusa makes a brief statement of great interest in its bearing on the evolution of the Zen-style garden: "In the past, outcasts (*kawaramono*) have been permitted in the imperial palace to do gardening; but, since these people are unclean, as of last year such permission is no longer granted. This year, among the menial laborers, only those of the class called *shomoji* will be employed in palace gardening."

Actually both *kawaramono* and *shomoji* belonged to a variegated lower class of people forced to do menial labor in lieu of paying taxes; the latter, however, were slightly higher up the social ladder. *Kawaramono* were people (*mono*) who lived in the bed (*kawara*) of the Kamo River or (in much smaller numbers) the Katsura River. The lowliness of their status resulted from their work: skinning horses and cows and tanning the hides for armor. Traffic in animal skins was abhorred because Buddhism forbids killing. The *shomoji*, however, who made their livings by going from door to door and reciting sutras for the good fortune of the inhabitants, were a step above ordinary beggars. This distinction excluded the *kawaramono* from garden work in the palace; the *shomoji*, untainted by the association with dead things, were allowed in.

Both of these classes were from ancient times subordinate to the stone-setting priests described earlier. Their very existence finds no mention in history until 1424, when a work called the *Kanmon nikki* describes their going to the aristocratic and temple gardens of Kyoto requisitioning trees for the garden of the imperial palace. Indeed, it may have been the unheard-of entry into the palace on just such an errand by members of the *kawaramono* class that prompted the edict forbidding their presence in that sacrosanct place.

Later, however, members of this lowly despised class were to become respected garden designers and specialists, ultimately to supplant the stone-setting priests who preceded them. It was in large part the power of the Zen

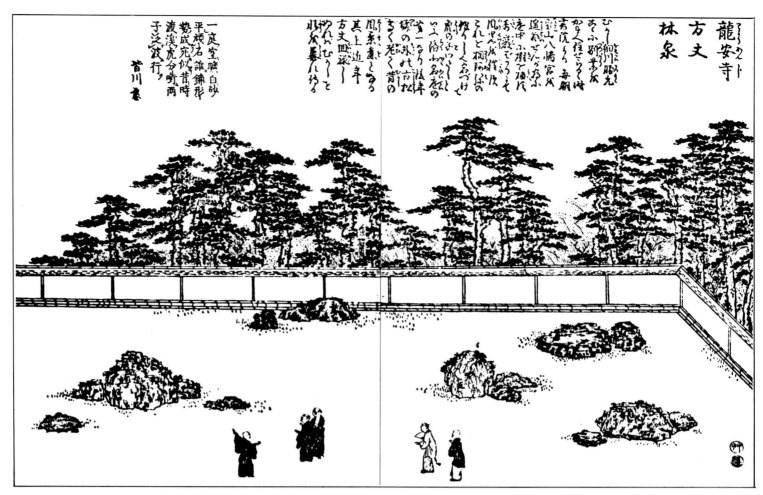

龍安寺 方丈 林泉

Ryōan-ji, Kyoto. (From an Edo-period guidebook.)

priests, who became their patrons and guides in Zen philosophy, that enabled them to effect this transformation.

The achievements of a leather worker named Matashirō is an illuminating case in point. One day, Matashirō said to a certain priest from the important Zen temple Shōkoku-ji: "With all my heart, I lament having been born into a leather-worker's family." To improve his social standing he set out to master the art of garden design and make gardens that would be praised for their creative imagination. He studied the pertinent works of history and landscaping and Buddhist philosophy, and was able to sell his gardening theories to influential and powerful clients.

A priest named Ranpa, of the residential subtemple Senkan-in at the Nanzen-ji, the most prestigious Zen temple in Kyoto, asked Matashirō how to revive a tree that seemed about to wither and die. Matashirō told the priest to write on paper a quotation from the twenty-fifth chapter of the Lotus Sutra: "Poured on them, the nectar rain of the Law eliminates all the delusions that obstruct the path to enlightenment." Buried at the roots, this paper would revive the tree without fail. In another temple in Kyoto, Matashirō constructed a waterfall in the southwest corner of the site and led the water from there to a stream flowing west to east. All gardening theories from the distant past had taught that streams are auspiciously oriented only if they flow from the east or the northeast. When asked why he had selected the opposite orientation, Matashirō said it was permitted because the Law of the Buddha was said to rise in the west and extend its influence gradually eastward. This assertion is in fact groundless, but the Zen priests must have been astounded to hear an outcast quoting the sutras and other Buddhist teachings. Indeed, they so respected this man that in 1504 Keijo Shūrin, a noted scholar and head priest of the Shōkoku-ji, conferred on him the honor of a Buddhist name: Jifuku.

People like Matashirō were handicapped not only by

their social standing, but also by having no access to the secret written traditions handed down from generation to generation that proved the authenticity of the stone-setting priests. Denied these traditions, the outcast gardeners of this period were compelled to create their own, which had to be more distinctively creative than anything that had gone before them. In this task they called on the assistance of the Zen priests—who became their patrons and philosophical mentors. The style born of cooperation between these two groups is called *kare sansui*, literally, "withered mountains and water" but better referred to as "dry landscape" or "stone-and-gravel" gardens.

The first outcast to became a respected gardener working in this tradition was Zen'ami (1386–1482). Zen'ami was not actually his given name, which is now unknown, but a Buddhist appellation granted him and used in connection with garden work. The *-ami* is a kind of title conferred by the Jishū Buddhist sect, which any person of low class who wished to work for the shogun, the aristocracy, or the high-ranking clergy had to have. Obviously craftsmen, poets, art critics, and other people playing important roles in the newly emerging culture of the time were eager to have names with *-ami* appended. Their interest in these names was practical, not religious; many who received names from the Jishū sect actually professed belief in some other form of Buddhism. Nor were the names conferred gratis. The prospective recipient had to master Buddhist teachings and be proficient in writing and calligraphy. In addition, he had to pass a kind of oral examination, and ultimately make donation of a large amount of money. The fact that Zen'ami had such a name, and that the name survived in written records, means that by the time he received it he was already a well-established, influential garden designer.

Zen'ami's greatest patron was the shogun Ashikaga Yoshimasa (1436–90). Yoshimasa's own position was entirely symbolic and devoid of all political power, but from his youth he was devoted to the new arts and culture

Ashikaga Yoshimasa.

he saw evolving around him. When he was first commissioned by the shogun to do garden work, Zen'ami was seventy-three; Yoshimasa was twenty-two. It may have been precisely because Zen'ami was an outcast living in a riverbed with refugees from peasant uprisings, where corpses were abandoned in times of famine (as many as 80,000 during the Kanshō famine of 1460–66), and because the shogun himself was politically impotent, that the two men were able to come together in this way. It is difficult to imagine what thoughts may have run through Zen'ami's head as he pondered garden designs in his riverbed home, surrounded by wretchedness and death.

Zen'ami's work includes many designs or redesigns for the residential subtemples of the shogunal family temple Shōkoku-ji, and for many other similar institutions associated with the shogun or the aristocracy in and around Kyoto and Nara: the shogunal residence (1459), the Daijō-in abbot's residence (1460), the Suiin-ken abbot's residence (1466), the Onryō-ken abbot's residence (1458), and the Chū-in abbot's residence (1471).

Despite the title conferred on him, Zen'ami was still a social outcast and was required to live in the areas relegated to such people. Violating this regulation once got him into considerable trouble. When he was working on the Daijō-in garden in Nara, part of the great temple of Kōfuku-ji, he was assigned a house that was not in the outcast ghetto. At the time, a kind of caste system maintained in the ten outcast districts of Nara, none of which was prepared to house a *kawaramono*—the lowest of the low. It became necessary to build a small house for Zen'ami on a piece of vacant land in the town. The priest-warriors attached to the Kōfuku-ji took umbrage at this and attacked, fully intending to raze Zen'ami's house to the ground. The fact that he was working for the Kōfuku-ji at the time mitigated in his favor, and the situation was smoothed over.

In 1476, at the age of ninety-one, Zen'ami reached the pinnacle for a person of his station and calling when he

was commissioned to design part of the south garden of the imperial palace. It is true that other *kawaramono* had designed gardens for people in very high places: the garden of a palace for the retired emperor in 1430, for example, and the waterfall and stone arrangements of a garden for imperial prince Fushimi no Miya Sadafusa in the early fifteenth century. But Zen'ami was the first to do this kind of work for a reigning emperor on such an important site as the imperial palace south garden, considered a place of the loftiest dignity. The preeminent role in gardening had passed from the stone-setting priests to the formerly despised outcasts.

A number of interesting questions arise about the relation between gardening and gardeners and Zen priests. Why did these clerics take interest in an activity that carried with it the inevitable need to dig about in the dirt, and was thus considered fit at best for low-ranking priests?

One contributory factor is the Zen attitude toward all actions. In the Zen view, everything a person does—eating, cleaning, bathing, evacuating, drinking tea, and gardening as well—can become a spiritual discipline. The arts are all forms of religious training, too, and no meaningful distinction is to made among them. Just as flowers, trees, stones, fish, and birds are all the Buddha in various forms, so floral and bird paintings, landscaping, and other forms of pictorial and sculptural art are Buddhist art. Zen does away with the distinction between religious and secular, and the image of the Buddha enshrined in the temple hall becomes for the Zen priest merely a formality. Priests who designed gardens considered this a part of their religious life.

Musō Soseki (1275–1351), for example, a Zen priest of high rank—the title by which he is also known, *kokushi* or "national teacher," was conferred by the emperor only upon the very few—designed several important gardens. An entry for 1344 in the diary of a noted Shingon priest and scholar named Kōhō (1306–62) criticizes him for engaging in work below his station, but Musō Soseki would have

Zen'ami's pond at Daijō-in, Nara.

insisted that all work in the secular world reveals the Buddha.

The desire to go beyond sensual beauty and to make a philosophical statement is another thing that prompted Zen priests to turn their hands to garden design. In the single-minded pursuit of universal principles, Zen gardens strip all nonessentials from nature and strive to discover the transcendent meaning of life. Materials are reduced to stones, gravel, and the occasional pruned planting (of shrubs such as tea, azalea, and sasanqua). The stones stand for the framework of the universal order, and the gravel symbolizes the cruel transience of this world. Because truths of this kind were their goal, designers of Zen gardens paid no attention to the sizes of the plots they had to work with: the small space between two buildings was just as significant for them as a great open zone.

Still another factor inspiring Zen priests to undertake work of this kind was the availability of skilled workmen in the presence of the *kawaramono* who, in the fourteenth and fifteenth centuries, after long years of work with the stone-setting priests, were ready to initiate a splendid flowering in garden culture. Seeing Zen'ami's garden for the Suiin-ken abbot's residence, the priest Kikei Shinzui had the most lavish of praise: "Viewing the small artificial mountain," he wrote, "I experienced a strange marvelous feeling. Gazing at it tirelessly, I forgot all about going home." Others said that for garden arrangements of all kinds Zen'ami was peerless; because there were people like him, the shogun, and the aristocracy, also became patrons of this class of outcasts.

Beyond his admiration for garden design, the shogun Yoshimasa had an extraordinarily deep affection for Zen'ami himself. When the old man grew seriously ill between 1460 and 1463, Yoshimasa often sent people to take him medicines or to console him, inquired after his needs, and expressed a longing to see him back at work again. It was virtually unheard of for a shogun to devote such care to a person of such humble origins. The priest Shinzui, however captivated he was by the Suiin-ken garden, was less kindly disposed to the relationship between these two men. "The shogun's compassion toward Zen'ami," he commented, "goes beyond the gardener's station and can even be called abnormal."

MOTION AND ADAPTATION

A general misconception prevails about the nature of the tea ceremony, which attained very much the form it has today during the sixteenth century—a time of great civil strife in Japan. It is usually thought that the tea ceremony is no more than a ceremonious, formalized way to drink tea. But this is only one of its many aspects. Actually, the proper conduct of a tea ceremony demands that the host educate himself thoroughly in a wide range of interests: the ceremony itself, art and craft appreciation, cooking, the display of the confections served during the ceremony, flower arranging, and the design of the buildings and gardens in which the ceremony takes place.

The Zen philosophy on which the tea ceremony is based maintains that everything a person does can be regarded as religious. As the Zen priest Ikkyū Sōjun (1394–1481) said, "the Buddha exists in the tea ceremony." It must be remembered, however, that there are a number of subsects of Zen Buddhism and that not all of them are associated with tea. The temple Daitoku-ji in Kyoto, where there are still a large number of tea-ceremony pavilions and where Ikkyū became abbot, was the most closely connected with the tea ceremony. The famous Zen temple Myōshin-ji, also in Kyoto, at first rejected the tea ceremony altogether, though in the Edo period (1615–1868) it was practiced there to a certain extent.

The tea-ceremony pavilion is not the only locale required for the ceremony itself. First there must be a garden that ushers the invited guests to the pavilion, with a basin and water for ritual purification of hands and mouth. This garden must provide an atmosphere consonant with participation in the tea ceremony. The second setting is a

Kaiseki meal: rice, miso soup, sashimi, vegetable.

Sen no Rikyū.

relatively spacious room, floored with tatami and fitted with a *tokonoma* (ornamental alcove) and an adjacent set of staggered shelves where a small number of decorative objects may be put on display. In this room the host serves his guests the so-called *kaiseki* meal consisting of various foods in requisite arrangements. The third setting is the tea-ceremony room itself, usually quite small, where the host serves tea to his guests and joins them in pleasant conversation. Though they have doors and windows, these pavilions are designed to have no direct view of the garden at all.

This lack of emphasis on the view stems from a characteristic distinguishing the tea-ceremony garden from other garden forms: people must walk through it to reach the tea-ceremony pavilion, and it is designed with this purpose in mind. The ceremony is considered to have begun the minute the guest enters this garden, which is most often arranged to evoke the mood of a remote, mysterious valley and to provide the visitor with a variety of delights to the eye as he passes along. For the people of

the time, living as they did in crowded cities, the beauty to be discovered in the narrow, twisting tea garden was especially prized. It was an artificial beauty, however, calculated to look as natural as possible. An anecdote about Sen no Rikyū (1522–91), a merchant of the free port of Sakai, not far from modern Osaka, and the greatest figure in the history of the tea ceremony, illustrates the point: it is said that one day after he had thoroughly swept and cleaned his tea garden in preparation for the arrival of his guests, he deliberately shook the boughs of the trees to bring down a clutter of more dry leaves.

The tea-ceremony garden was the first in Japanese history to take walking into consideration in its composition, and in fact is called a *roji*—"passageway" or "alley." With the exception of special gardens for heads of tea-ceremony schools, the roji is never a main garden but is most often constructed in narrow spaces between buildings and fences. The important thing about it is the influence it has on the minds of those who walk through it and discover beauty in a sequence of experiences.

Tea-room tokonoma with winter display of hanging scroll and camellia.

Material for making tea: kettle, cloth, tea leaves.

To help create the right mood of cleanliness and freshness, the host always sprinkles the roji with water before his guests arrive. Timing is of the essence. The wetness of stones and ground is a sign to guests that they may enter. If the ceremony is to be held during the day, however, freshly watered grounds would have less than the desired effect; the host thus sprinkles the roji well in advance, so that it is about a third dry when guests appear. The custom is somewhat different for ceremonies held at night. Even today electric lighting is never used in the roji; the flickering light of candles is preferred. The candles are set in suitable lanterns staggered on both sides of the garden path; heavy sprinkling transforms the trees and stones—everything in the garden—into a world of fantasy unlike anything to be experienced in ordinary life.

The roji is usually small, but its influence on the history of Japanese gardening has been enormous. The roles of movement and sequential experience are only two of its innovations; another is the idea of using to aesthetic advantage things originally intended for other purposes, or

things that people have discarded or overlooked. Stones found by the roadside, jars of the kind used in ordinary farmhouses, and damaged or imperfectly fired tea bowls were all objects that a sensitivity to the simple, slightly melancholy, refined beauty conveyed by the Japanese words *wabi* and *sabi* could convert into priceless treasures of art and craftsmanship. Great discernment was of course essential in choosing objects with such potential value from those that were merely run-of-the-mill.

This philosophy of adapting things to new uses is well illustrated in the fate of stone lanterns and stepping stones. Votive lamps donated by the faithful to Buddhist temples and Shinto shrines did not become garden elements until the late sixteenth century. Probably in about 1580, Sen no Rikyū became intrigued by the stone lanterns in the bleak Toribeno cemetery, on the outskirts of Kyoto, and decided to use them in his tea gardens. The first recorded instance of such usage, however, is a reference to three stone lanterns in the Osaka tea garden of wealthy merchant and tea ceremony aficionado Tsuda Sōkyū (d. 1591); the

Tea garden and tea-room entrance at Urasenke, Kyoto.

Courtyard garden at Fukami Residence, Kyoto.

reference occurs in one of the customary written accounts of a tea ceremony held there on October 24, 1590. A similar record for October 4, 1591 mentions a stone lantern in the tea garden of one Dōga of a shop called Ogaya, in Nara. It may be assumed from these records that such lanterns were already growing in popularity. It is one of the ironies of history that this usage, which originated with Sen no Rikyū, was finding increasing acceptance at just the time when his lord and patron Toyotomi Hideyoshi (1536–98) ordered Rikyū to commit ritual suicide. In any case, the stone lantern has lost all religious connotation in the tea-garden setting, and has become a means of illumination for evening gatherings and a decorative addition to the daytime landscape.

Like the stone lantern, found in practically all traditional Japanese gardens, stepping stones are another example of creative adaptation and were originally limited to tea-ceremony gardens. They were no doubt initially used in connection with the sequential experience of a walk through the roji. From the practical viewpoint, stepping stones orient the guest in his movement through the garden and help keep his feet clean. From the aesthetic viewpoint, they are important to the overall mood—pleasing to the eye in the moss or gravel of the ground cover, in the water of a stream or pond, or in the snow. In garden terminology, the practical aspect of stepping stones is called *watari* ("pass-over"), and the aesthetic aspect *kei* ("scene"). Garden designers differ in the relative importance they assign the two in placing the stones: Sen no Rikyū, for example, allotted 60 percent importance to *watari*, function, and 40 percent to *kei*, beauty; his pupil Furuta Oribe (1544–1615) reversed those percentages.

To traverse a stepping stone path without mishap, the visitor must not allow his attention to be diverted by the scenery around him. Tea gardens are designed to help concentrate the attention on the business of walking on the stones; to provide a breather, however, midcourse in

the path there will often be a particularly large stone—as big as 1.5 meters in diameter—inviting the visitor to pause and take a look around him. The walk from the garden gate to the first large stone, and then to either the next large stone or the tea-ceremony pavilion itself, is like a flight from one airport to another and then to another: each pause in the journey introduces the traveler to new, often surprising, experiences. Frequently, post-foundation stones from ruined temples or monasteries were used for this purpose in tea gardens, but at present the number of such stones is out of all proportion to the number of ruined temples. Obviously, most of them are copies.

In the seventeenth century, people began building gardens based on the roji design on small plots of land attached to their townhouses. With the usual basin for ritual ablutions, stone lanterns, stepping stones, plants, and so on, these domestic versions looked like tea-ceremony gardens but were actually designed to be seen and enjoyed from inside the house and to provide natural illumination and ventilation. All small gardens of this kind, with the exception of the few that were actually used for tea-ceremony purposes, are called *tsuboniwa*. They were usually constructed in small square plots enclosed by the wings of the house, where the lighting and ventilation were not right for a true roji, but their growing popularity among the common people indicates how powerful a cultivating and educating force the tea ceremony was.

MUTE MUSICAL PATHWAYS

There were two major categories of clients for the numerous gardens created in a new style in the first part of the seventeenth century. First were the imperial court and the aristocracy, who, in 1617, when the Tokugawa shogunate was in control of the nation, were instructed to confine their activities to the pursuit of arts and leisure and, by implication, to stay out of politics. Second were the feudal lords loyal to the shogunate and possessed of considerable political power.

Courtyard garden using tea-garden elements at Sugimoto Residence, Kyoto.

These gardens for strolling, as they are called, were often vast. The Toyama-sō, for example, constructed between 1661 and 1672, was the Edo villa of the Owari branch of the Tokugawa clan; it is recorded to have covered 136,400 *tsubo* or about 450,000 square meters.

The retired emperor Gomizuno-o (1596–1680) was responsible for the construction of a large number of gardens in and around Kyoto. The two most famous surviving examples are the Shugakuin Detached Palace (1659) on a hillside northeast of Kyoto, characterized by its use of ancient garden design techniques, and the Sentō Palace (1630) near the imperial compound, comprising two linked ponds. As we have noted, the idea of incorporating the effect of movement—specifically walking—in garden design was first evolved for the small tea-ceremony garden. Larger gardens for strolling carry this approach a step farther and are designed to allow visitors to walk around the shores of the pond or lake—which they invariably include—and to enjoy the changing vistas as they go.

Of course, garden sauntering was no novelty. It had long been the custom in any landscaped area that was big enough—especially in the gardens designed as re-creations of paradise on earth. In such cases, however, the garden was the realm of the Buddha; though he was only mortal, as long as the visitor was in such a place, he was—in principle at any rate—a Buddha. Mortals might hold poetry parties, boat excursions, or theatrical performances in them, but the paradise gardens were first and foremost of the spiritual world; the stroller was not merely walking about the garden for pleasure but moving from one to another of the chapellike buildings in it, intoning prayers before each.

It was Zen philosophy that rid the garden of its deep religious overtones. Since all the phenomena of nature represented forms of the Buddha, worship halls and chapels were superfluous. When this idea gained acceptance, religion left the garden. Buddhist halls and Shinto shrines are frequently found in gardens for strolling of the later

period; no longer objects of religious faith or worship, however, they are only features in the landscape.

Other facets of these gardens may also be traced to earlier influences. For instance, artificial hillocks, ponds with islands, water courses, and stones set in flat areas or on the shores of the pond all derive from ancient gardens. Arrangements of stones with raked gravel and a minimum of pruned shrubbery belong to the Zen garden tradition of the fifteenth century; stone lanterns, stepping stones, and ritual water basins trace their ancestry to the tea-ceremony gardens of the sixteenth century.

The oldest surviving garden for strolling is that of the Katsura Detached Palace, built between 1620 and 1640 as a retreat by imperial prince Hachijō Toshihito and his son Toshitada. The appellation "detached palace" does not indicate that any emperor ever resided in the villa. It simply means the whole establishment is the property of the imperial household. In 1881, the Hachijō line died out, and five years later Katsura became a possession of the Ministry of the Imperial Household—now the Imperial Household Agency.

The Katsura pond, fed by waters from the old course of the nearby Katsura River, is surrounded by paths: some of these are made of stepping stones, some of strips of stone pavement; some are spread with gravel, some are modified into stone staircases, and some are bare ground. Along the paths are garden elements of three kinds: small rustic bowers for resting or the reception of guests, including the Shōkin-tei, the Shōka-tei, the Manji-tei, the Shōiken, and the Gepparō; miniaturizations of famous scenic attractions including the Sumiyoshi pine, the Tsutsumi waterfall, the Ōigawa river, and the famous wooded sand spit called Ama no Hashidate; and artistic stone objects including a series of stone lanterns—the Mizu-hotaru lantern, whose light flickering on the surface of the pond resembled a host of fireflies (*hotaru*), the Yukimi ("snow-viewing") lantern, designed to look especially good in winter, and the Sankō lantern, with three (*san*) windows around its light

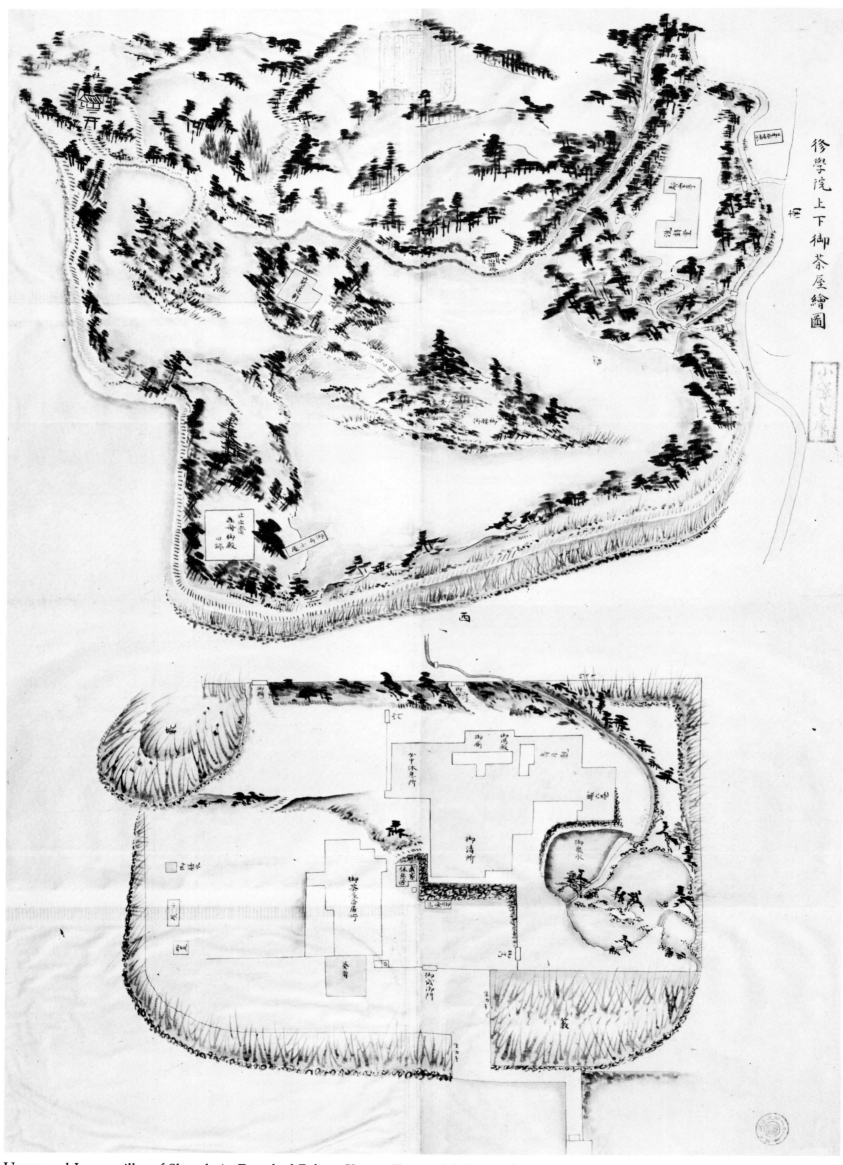

修學院上下御茶屋繪圖

西

Upper and Lower villas of Shugakuin Detached Palace, Kyoto. (From a Meiji-period map.)

Stone pavement and stepping stones before Imperial Entryway at Katsura Detached Palace, Kyoto.

compartment. All the hills, streams, plants, bridges, valleys, and so on in the garden have been assigned associations with classical poetry and such other works of Japanese literature as *The Tale of Genji*; visitors could enjoy composing poetry of their own inspired by the rich literary associations that are an integral part of the design.

If preceding garden styles had been pictorial—indeed paintings often inspired their creation—the garden for strolling is more aptly described as musical. This is primarily because, like the tea-ceremony garden, it incorporates the effects of motion. The designers of course gave careful thought to all the elements they placed on both sides of the paths, but an equally important part of the design is the play and manipulation of space as experienced by the visitor as he moves from a wide open space to a narrow one, from a region of bright light into gloom, from an expansive rural setting into a hilly region. Now the pond is visible; now it is concealed by hills and groves. Other visitors appear on the far side of the pond, from behind a stand of trees, and then disappear again. The result might be called mute music, with its own special

rhythms and variations. There seem to have been no specific rules about direction, but in general gardens of this kind are designed to be toured and observed in a certain order, and this also has something in common with the ordered sequence of music.

Gardens for strolling are notable for the amount of latitude the designers had in their work. They were built during a time when the government was so determined to protect the established feudal order that even the kinds of houses people in each social class could build for themselves were rigidly prescribed. But as long as they did nothing to violate the basic conditions of that feudal order, gardens for strolling could be designed however the owners wished. Whether the owners were members of the court aristocracy or feudal lords, such gardens were almost always built in retreats or villas where this latitude and freedom must have been a very welcome relief from the punctilious ceremony that, in those days, hung like a heavy burden around the neck of anyone with any kind of position at all.

Fortunately, throughout most of the Edo period Japan

Murin-an stroll garden, Kyoto.

was at peace. The samurai ceased to be a fighting man and became a civil administrator. Court aristocrats, shut out of politics, had the leisure to devote themselves to cultural pursuits—one of which was the untrammeled creative design of gardens for strolling. The shogunate was happy to indulge them in this pastime, which it viewed as no threat to the established system.

Some of the most famous extant gardens of the genre are the Kōraku-en of the Mito branch of the Tokugawa clan, the Toyama-sō of the Owari branch, the Yokuon-en of the Shirakawa branch of the Matsudaira clan, the Rikugi-en of the Kōfu branch of the Yanagisawa clan, and the Tokugawa shogun's Hama Palace. All of these are in the Tokyo area. Noted gardens for strolling in other parts of the country include the Ritsurin Park of the Takamatsu branch of the Matsudaira clan, the Kōraku-en of the

Okayama branch of the Ikeda clan, the Kenroku-en of the Kanazawa branch of the Maeda clan, and the Jōju-en of the Kumamoto branch of the Hosokawa clan.

The first steps in the development of modern Japan were taken in 1868, when the Tokugawa shogunate gave up all political power into the hands of the Meiji imperial court. With modernization and Westernization came the introduction of Western garden styles, but given the way the Japanese have always responded to cultural importations, this did not spell the instant demise of the garden for strolling. On the contrary, a considerable number were created in the latter part of the nineteenth century; the Murin-an and Shinshin-an gardens in the vicinity of the Zen temple Nanzen-ji in Kyoto are only two examples. The only thing to change in this connection was ownership.

The temple Saihō-ji maintains one of Kyoto's most popular gardens, with a pristine forest and still pond set in mossy banks that are lush, cool, and green. So splendid is the moss here that the Japanese people prefer their own name for the place: they call it Koke-dera, the Moss Temple. But where did the moss come from?

THE MOSS TEMPLE

Entrance pathway. The visitor does not enter the garden directly but skirts its perimeter on a long straight pathway. The foliage beyond the high wall heightens the anticipation of what lies ahead.

Log bridge crossing to main island. The most distinctive feature of Saihō-ji is the moss, thus the popular name Koke-dera, or Moss Temple. The moist clay soil and shady location have fostered its luxuriant growth. According to one count, there are about forty different species here.

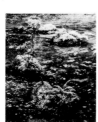

Inlet with mooring stones. The lower garden contains a large pond, excavated long ago as part of a depiction of the Buddhist Western Paradise. Centuries later it was used as a site for boating—the photograph shows what may have been mooring stones—and viewing cherry blossoms and autumn leaves. By the end of the seventeenth century, Saihō-ji was in ruins.

View of pond from main island. The pristine state of Saihō-ji today—the velvety softness of the moss and the unobstructed view through the trees—makes this garden a wonderland of enchantment. It is easy to feel a little sad as one accepts its quiet, delicate beauty. This emotion is often expressed in Japanese art, but nowhere is it so tangibly enacted as here.

Dry cascade of the upper garden. The upper garden is completely different in mood from the pond garden below. Here the rockwork dominates, and there is a latent, powerful energy in the arrangement. The use of flat, low-lying stones was to predominate in later centuries.

"Sugi" moss around a stepping stone. Here and below: mosses found at Saihō-ji.

"Mōsen" moss around a root.

"Saihō-ji" moss near a stream.

Camellia flowers and "hosoba okina" moss.

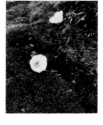

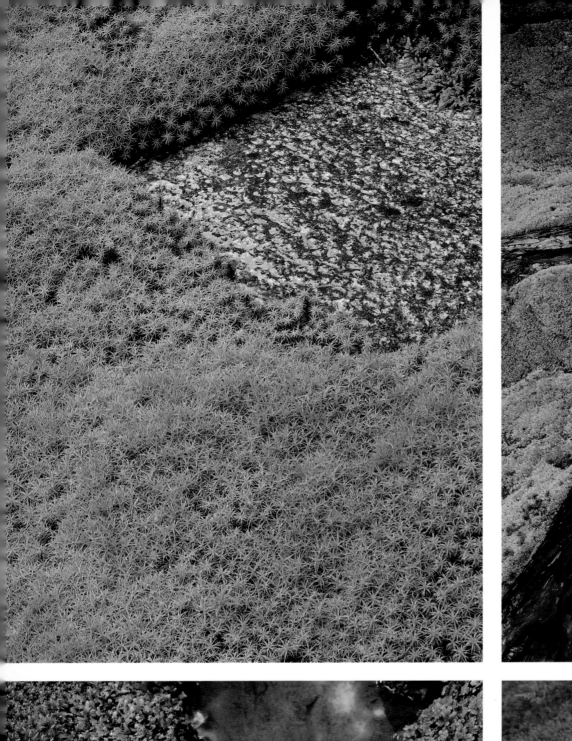
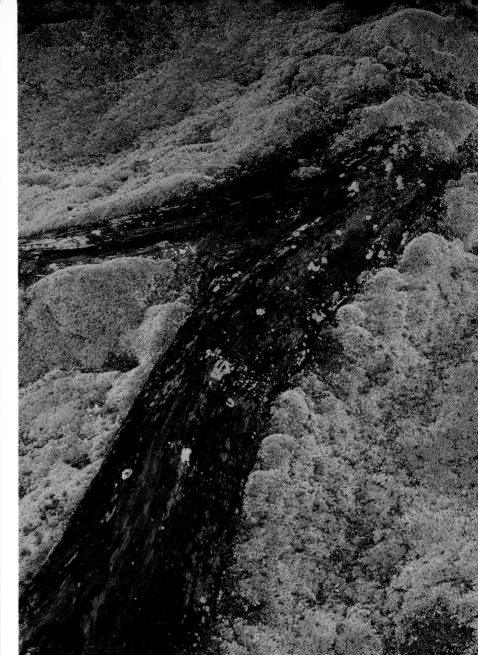

CONFINED NOW
TO FANTASY

Saihō-ji, as it might have looked in early times. Screen painting by Hisatsune Shūji (1960).

The Zen priest Musō Soseki (1275–1351) created the garden of the Saihō-ji—popularly called the Koke-dera or Moss Temple—in 1339, at a time when Japan had two rival imperial courts: the Northern court supported by the Ashikaga shogunate and based in Kyoto, and the Southern court, located on Mount Yoshino. Very little remains today to indicate what that garden, considered rare and original in its time, looked like then. It is now a quiet, somber place with murmuring streams, stone groupings that look as if they had been dug from the earth and left as they were, and velvety moss covering the ground under the trees. The buildings blend into the natural setting. In the autumn, when red and brown leaves presage the death of the year, the occasional call of a bird has more of silence than of song about it.

The only hints we have about the appearance of the garden in its days of glory are the unchanged location on the lower slopes of Mount Torigatake; the Saihō-ji River flowing through the valley; the Golden Pond, a name that

belies its somber appearance; and stone groupings that preserve a certain harmony, though it is no longer possible to say whether they were deliberately planned or fortuitous.

Aside from the small tea-ceremony house called the Shōnan-tei, built by the tea master Sen no Shōan between 1596 and 1614, none of the buildings go back before 1887. In short, the garden of the Saihō-ji as it was created in the fourteenth century now belongs solely to the realm of fantasy.

In the past, as was often the case in Buddhist monasteries and temples, women were not allowed in the compound of the Saihō-ji. The rule applied even to so high-placed a lady as the mother of the Ashikaga shogun Yoshimasa (1436–90), and to gratify her desire to see the garden that people praised so enthusiastically, Yoshimasa had a copy of it made at his own villa, the Ginkaku-ji. Now, however, the Saihō-ji is a tourist temple visited by members of both sexes. They see something not very far

101

The garden at Ginkaku-ji, modeled on Saihō-ji.

Saihō-ji: Golden Pond.

Musō Soseki.

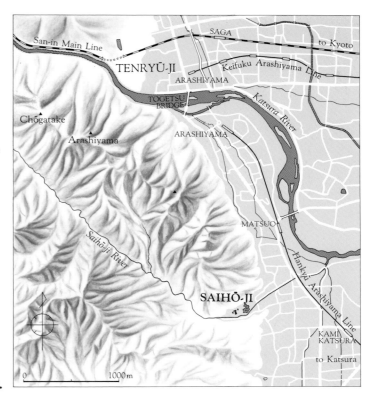
Map of Saihō-ji vicinity.

Tenryū-ji. (From an Edo-period guidebook.)

from pristine nature in appearance, but the original garden was a highly artificial composition based on Musō Soseki's Zen philosophy, as documents of the day reveal.

IN SPITE OF WAR AND RANK

The fourteenth century was one of strife between the Northern and Southern courts. The conservative Southern court lived in virtual defeat on Mount Yoshino but had one consolation: it possessed the Imperial Regalia, the jewel, sword, and mirror that are the three holy symbols of the legitimacy of the Japanese imperial house. The much more progressive Northern court maintained its superiority from its headquarters in the capital city. Each court served its own emperor.

The Zen priest Musō Soseki lived and worked in Kyoto, which was under the control of the Northern court. He petitioned the shogun Ashikaga Takauji (1305–58), however, to build a temple to pray for the spirits of the Southern emperor, Godaigo (d. 1339), and the warriors loyal to him who had died in battle. Permission was granted, and construction of the Tenryū-ji (initially called the Ryakuō-ji) was completed in 1345. Funds for the

project came largely from the profits of a renewed trade with China; the merchant vessels involved in this trade came to be called "Tenryū-ji ships." The temple was built on the grounds of the Kameyama mansion, which had close associations with the emperor Godaigo. The gardens and the building were constructed and completed at the same time. During the work on the garden, Musō Soseki dug earth himself and carried it in bamboo baskets to the front of the temple hall as the initial ceremony marking the establishment of the new temple.

Much remains to show us today what the garden originally looked like: the waterfall called Sankyoku, on the middle slope of Kameyama hill; the Sōgen pond, the Banshō cave in its grove of pines; and stone groupings designed to recall the mountains in the ink landscape paintings of the Chinese Song dynasty (960–1279). From the Tenryū-ji it is possible to see the hill Arashiyama and the cherry and maple trees that Ashikaga Takauji had had planted there in memory of his enemy. (Because Godaigo, while dreaming of a return to the capital, died on Mount Yoshino, which is famous for its cherry trees. War in the Japan of this time was cruel and bloody, as war

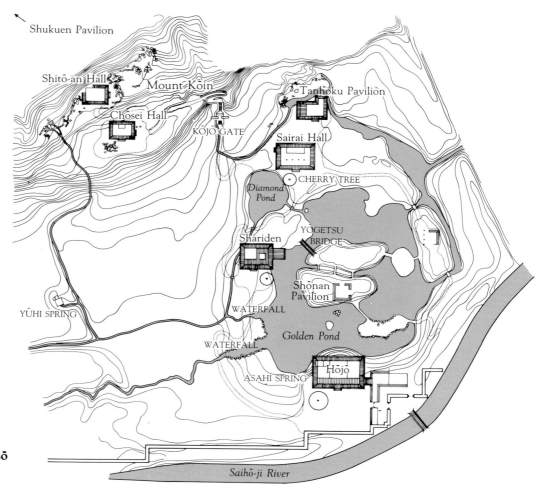

Map of Saihō-ji at the time of Musō Soseki. (Based on the research of Nishizawa Fumitaka.)

always is. Buddhism taught that all people become Buddhas when they die. It is not especially odd, then, that the victor Ashikaga should have gone to great lengths to pay homage to the spirit of his dead enemy. Is it because there is no postmortem distinction between friend and foe that in Japanese history war has generally seemed to be a kind of ceremonial accompanied by bloodshed?)

Despite his own high clerical rank and the warfare that disrupted the Japan of his day, Musō Soseki designed gardens for many temples that were being either established or restored. Though he was despised by some for doing what they considered degrading labor, he undertook this work as a kind of Zen discipline and training. The Tenryū-ji was being built at just the time when the Saihō-ji was being restored; since the two are only about a kilometer apart, he was able to go back and forth between them, executing distinctive and original garden designs in both at the same time.

WORLDS PURE AND PROFANE

The land on which the Saihō-ji stands was the site of an earlier temple with a name phonetically the same; written with different Chinese characters, however, that name meant the Temple of the Western Paradise. The Saihō-ji was a Zen temple, but its predecessor belonged to the Pure Land sect, which teaches that merely calling on the name of the Buddha Amida ensures entry into Sukhavati—the Western Paradise. Naturally, the garden of the older temple was a temporal reconstruction of that realm; the pond in the Saihō-ji today was originally a so-called Pond of the Seven Precious Substances, typical of such gardens. By Musō Soseki's day, however, the temple compound was in desolation; nothing remained to indicate what the original Saihō-ji had been like.

The garden today is divided into two major regions: the flat area, with the pond; and the hilly region called Mount Kōin, strewn with projecting boulders. The flat region stands for the world of tranquillity, of paradise, and of life;

the rough, stony region (originally the site of a temple called the Edo-ji) represents the present world in all its defilement. Indeed, at one time burials and services for the dead were held there.

Musō Soseki undertook the reconstruction of the Saihō-ji on commission from an important shogunal official named Fujiwara no Chikahide (1288–1341), who donated lands to the temple to repair its finances. It was at about this time that the Saihō-ji passed from the Pure Land to the Zen sect, and was put under joint administration with the Edo-ji; that is, the temple of the Pure Land and the temple of the profane present were amalgamated. In his work called Muchū mondō Musō Soseki writes: "It is delusion to think that the pure world of paradise and the profane world of the present are different. The distinction between holy purity and defilement, too, is delusion. Both are only groundless imaginings that spring into the human mind." He also believed that the philosophy of the Buddha is one in whatever sect it was professed and, on a plot of land formerly devoted to the Pure Land doctrine, had the pond reshaped to resemble the Chinese character for the word "mind," built halls and lodgings, and endowed the garden with fantastically shaped stones and trees in his own distinctive Zen style.

For a Zen temple, creating and maintaining a garden were important to overall appearances. Zen priests also regarded gardening as a kind of religious discipline. Musō Soseki seems to have had a purely personal interest in this kind of work, however, that transcended both these considerations. In a famous military saga called the Taiheiki, written about 1371, he is said to have had an innate ability to create gardens that invoked famous places, and a great natural affinity for stones and water. Another book called the Kaiki (1724–35) says that he had a very special curiosity about gardens.

For the Saihō-ji garden, he drew upon two philosophical sources. The first is the ten-fascicle Biyanlu from the Song dynasty in China, which in an annotated version has been

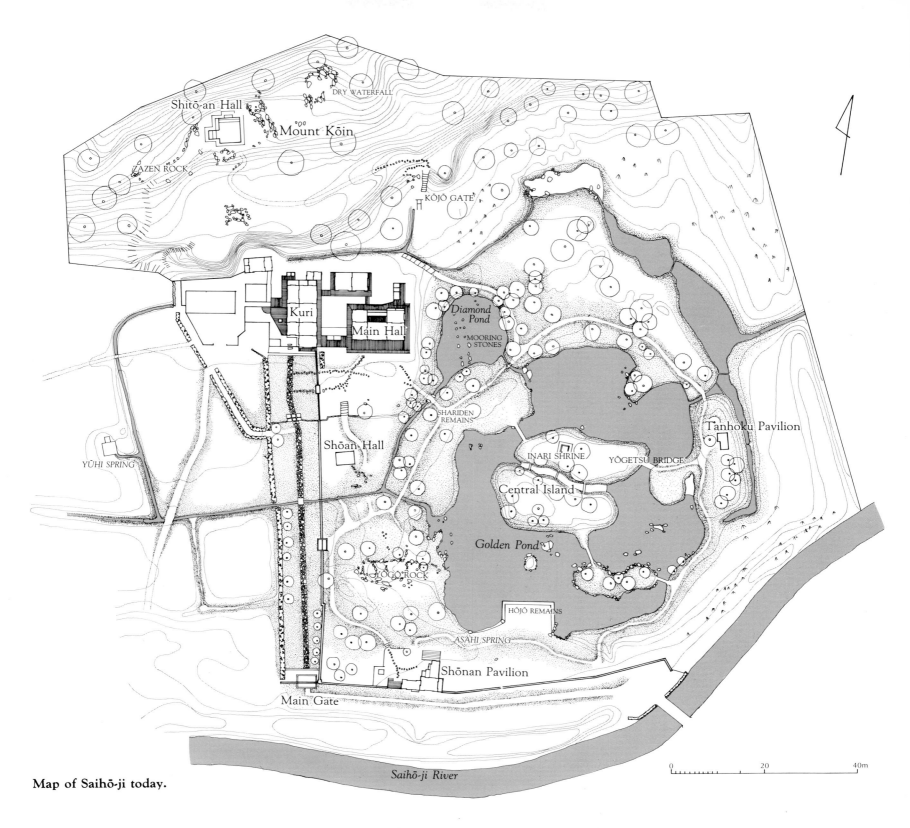

Map of Saihō-ji today.

Map labels: Shitō-an Hall · DRY WATERFALL · Mount Kōin · ZAZEN ROCK · KŌJŌ GATE · Kuri · Diamond Pond · MOORING STONES · Main Hall · SHARIDEN REMAINS · Tanhoku Pavilion · Shōan Hall · INARI SHRINE · YŌGETSU BRIDGE · YŪHI SPRING · Central Island · Golden Pond · ZOGO ROCK · HŌJŌ REMAINS · ASAHI SPRING · Shōnan Pavilion · Main Gate · Saihō-ji River · 0 · 20 · 40m

an instructional work of the greatest importance to Japanese Zen Buddhists, who call it the *Hekiganroku* (Record of the Blue Cliff). In it appears the following story.

The Tang emperor Diazong once asked the famous priest Nanyang what kind of respect he wanted paid to his memory after his death. Nanyang replied, "Erect a grave marker for me." The emperor was very puzzled, since it was common practice to erect such markers for priests of high rank and there was therefore no need to make a special request for one. When Nanyang observed the emperor shaking his head in puzzlement, he said that, if the request was not clear, he should ask Tanyuan—one of the priest's disciples—to interpret it for him after his death.

When Nanyang finally died, the emperor did as he was told; Tanyuan then explained that the memorial should extend "south of Xiang and north of Tan." In other words, Nanyang had asked for a memorial marker big enough to cover all the provinces of the Tang empire, and by extension the entire universe. Physically impossible, of course, the tower he meant was spiritual in nature. "A golden light," said Tanyuan, "will flood everything from south of Xiang to north of Tan, and there will be no

shadows under trees at noontime. Bathed in this golden radiance, all will be happy. The society of man will be like one great vessel. Among the lords and nobles in the palace of King Virudhaka of Shravasti, who slaughtered the Shakya tribe in Kapilavastu, there is no famous priest capable of understanding the true realm of the Law."

In this reply occur many terms that are incorporated as references in the Saihō-ji garden. Golden Pond refers to the golden light that will flood the universe when Nanyang's spiritual memorial marker is made manifest. The Shōnan-tei, one of the buildings in the garden, quotes the phrase "south of Xiang" (*shō* being the Japanese reading of the Chinese character *xiang*); another, called the Tanhoku-tei, means "north of Tan." The second floor of the Shariden, or Buddha-relics hall, was called Muhōtō, which is the name of the kind of grave marker Nanyang asked to have erected after his death; the first floor was called Ruriden, which is a Sino-Japanese rendition of the name of the palace of King Virudhaka. In the pond is a large stone representing the one great vessel that the prophecy says human society will come to resemble. Interestingly, the Buddha-relics hall became the model for the celebrated

The Golden Pavilion at Rokuon-ji.

gilded hall at the Temple of the Golden Pavilion: the Kinkaku-ji or, more correctly, the Rokuon-ji.

The upper garden, the one on the site of the Edo-ji representing the impure temporal world, derives its design from the story of an encounter between a man named Xiong Xiucai and a Ch'an (Zen) abbot named Liang. A mural by Shūi Mutō depicting the incident is said to have been on the wall of a small Buddha hall called the Shitō-an that once stood in this part of the garden.

In the reign of Zhenghe (1111–17), in the Song dynasty, a man named Xiong Xiucai made a trip to Mount Xishan in Hong province. As he was being carried up the mountain in a palanquin, a light rain fell dripping on him from the green leaves of the trees. At the end of his climb, he came upon an old white-haired priest seated on a stone. Xiong Xiucai said to the old man: "Today there are no good priests. I have heard that the famous abbot Liang secluded himself on this mountain. Perhaps you are that very same Liang." In reply, the old priest pointed eastward. Xiong Xiucai looked to the east, but when he turned around again the old man was gone. The surface of the stone where he had seen the old man sitting was dry, though rain had wet all the rest. Looking in all directions, Xiong Xiucai sighed and said: "I have met the abbot Liang, but it is as if I had not."

This anecdote is quoted in the upper section of the Saihō-ji garden in several ways. The name of the Shitō-an hall cited earlier means "pointing to the east." The stony mountain path and the trees recall the slopes of Xishan that Xiong Xiucai ascended in his palanquin, and the garden is accented with a stone called the Zazen, or "seated meditation," in reference to that on which Liang was seated.

Musō Soseki was apparently fond of the character in this tale. When he was asked by Fujiwara no Chikahide to undertake the restoration of the Saihō-ji, he replied: "I am happy to be able to live and work in a place that has the same name [western mountains, or *xishan* in Chinese] as

the one in Hong province associated with abbot Liang." The Saihō-ji is located in the mountains west of Kyoto.

STRANGE STONES, WEIRD TREES

Despite the lamentable lack of documentary evidence about the actual formation of the Saihō-ji garden, it is reasonable to assume that Musō Soseki used materials already on the site. The many craftsmen and laborers who must have helped Musō Soseki with the work piled the stones and other materials they collected in the vicinity of a willow tree said to have been planted on the old temple site by a famous Buddhist priest of the Nara period named Gyōki (668–749). A large cherry tree that had stood in front of the Amida hall when the temple belonged to the Pure Land sect played a part in the later garden as well. A verse by the Buddhist priest Bukkō Kokushi mentions the splendor of the magnificent maple trees. The pond in Pure Land garden style was reshaped, and water was conveyed to it by covered conduits to bubble forth from among the stones along the side.

It is also likely that stones once used to surround the burial chamber of a grave mound on the site were employed in the garden. The Yōgō stone symbolizing the Buddha's temporary appearance in the world to save sentient creatives, for example, and the Zazen stone in the upper part of the garden are said to have come from such a mound. The stone groupings in this region may have been artificially arranged or may simply have been left where digging uncovered them; it is difficult to be certain today which is the case.

The work involved in the creation of the garden brings to mind the legend of the Somedono Jizō. Jizō, or the bodhisattva Kshitagarbha, is thought to save sentient beings from suffering in this world and to guide the dead—especially children and people who were wicked—from hell. Jizō is usually represented as a tonsured priest, bearing a staff surmounted with a metal ornament and metal loops at the top. During the construction of the

Shōnan-tei.

Yōgō stone.

Saihō-ji garden, a strange priest appeared on the site and began moving great stones and transporting trees from one place to another. Soon the garden was finished; as a token that he had contributed to it the priest left his own staff there and demanded Musō Soseki's mantle. Not long thereafter it was reported that the statue of Jizō at the temple Somedono, in Kyoto Shijō, had lost its staff and gained a mantle.

It is possible that this legend arose because the making of the garden had disturbed an ancient burial mound, which yielded the abundance of stones in the upper region. In other words, the project had violated a resting place of the dead, and it was felt that introducing Jizō—the bodhisattva who looked after the spirits of the departed—might be some compensation for the intrusion.

On the completion of the temple a great ceremony was held in which fish and birds in the pond and trees of the garden were set free. Buddhism forbids the taking of life, and the freeing of living creatures was supposed to help human beings earn merit, offsetting the bad karma they incur by killing for sustenance. Present at the Saihō-ji ceremony were priests from the Kōmyō-ji, Nison-in, and Seika-ji temples. Purple clouds covered the sky; the eyes of the main image of the temple shown like the sun and the moon. The sands of the garden and the waters of the pond shown brilliantly as the fish and birds were released. But we know nothing more about what the garden was like at this important moment in its history, when the Saihō-ji was beginning its life as place of Zen training and discipline.

As time went by, however, a change came over the way the temple grounds were used. We know, for instance, that on March 26, 1349 the emperor Kōmyō stopped at the Saihō-ji after paying a visit to the temple Tenryū-ji. On this day, no Buddhist ceremonies were taking place. The emperor did no more than have a good time admiring the cherry flowers, listening to music, and riding in a boat on the pond. The high-minded Zen precepts on which Musō

Soseki had based the garden design were forgotten; people were interested solely in the beauty of the landscape. Indeed, the trend had started two years earlier when the emperor had come to go boating and enjoy the cherry trees at night by the light of ten tall candles. Serious religious training at the Saihō-ji had given way to temporal pleasures.

Part of the historical record are the impressions of two Koreans who visited Saihō-ji around this time. One is a short text by an envoy in a work picturesquely entitled *Hall of Ancient Pines: A Record of Travel in Japan.* He described the Saihō-ji, which he visited in 1420, in the following way:

> There are three islands in the pond in the east part of the temple grounds. On one island are blue pines, white sands, and an arbor. On the second is a small pavilion. The pavilion on the westernmost island is splendidly decorated with gems representing relics of the Buddha. Streams flow below flower-laden trees. Abundant fish swim in the pond, on whose surface ducks float. Small boats take visitors to the islands. On the banks of the ponds are thickets of pruned flowering plants.

The description of the garden made by a scribe with a diplomatic mission from Korea who was twenty-seven when he made his visit—on July 9, 1443—is much more detailed. He too came to the Saihō-ji, not for religious training, but for rest and to enjoy the garden in late summer. His description is long, and what follows are only the most salient points.

He observes, first, that while the names of the temple buildings derive from Chinese sources, the buildings themselves are constructed in an eclectic combination of Japanese and Chinese styles. Second, he notes that, unlike the gardens in the Heian manner, which recalled the

Zazen stone.

Site of ruined Shariden, or Buddhist-relics hall.

Steps leading up Mount Kōin.

yamato-e style of painting, the Saihō-ji garden contained strange stones, weird trees, and odd flowers. The branches of trees, for example, were tied with ropes to force them into the shapes the gardeners wanted; young trees were treated in such a way as to make them look old. Third, he remarks on the stand of pine and bamboo covering the hill behind the temple and notes that in the central part are planted flowering trees and maples. In the spring, one enjoys the flowers; in the summer, the cool stream and the greenery; and in the autumn, the splendid colors of the foliage. Fourth, he speaks of pruned, shaped plants, which may be the first mentioned in the history of Japanese gardening. Finally, he speaks of the large number of burial-mound stones, cast up from the earth and arranged in forms to be found in the works of neither man nor nature.

From all these comments it is possible to draw one conclusion: the garden of the Saihō-ji at this stage of its history was a combination of Chinese-style effects of color in its flowering plants and the bizarre effects of strange stones and weird trees. There was nothing in it, however, to justify the name "Moss Temple" that it bears today.

THE MOSSES

No other shogun visited the Saihō-ji as often as Ashikaga Yoshimasa, who went there twice yearly—in spring and fall—during the six years from 1436 to 1441. Between 1458 and 1466, he visited the temple fifteen times, once again mostly in spring and fall, probably because of some regularly scheduled events in these seasons. But if Zen was the pretext, enjoyment of the garden was no doubt the real aim of his frequent visits. On his visit in 1458, for example, he burned incense in the main Buddha hall, and in the Chosei-ken and Shitō-an halls; then he enjoyed the distant scenery from the Shukuen-tei arbor on the hill and took a boat ride on Golden Pond.

A visit to view the maples made by the shogun Ashikaga Yoshimitsu, on October 13, 1382, has been recorded in a diary by the Zen priest Gidō Shūshin. First, the shogun sat in silent meditation in memory of Musō Soseki in the Shitō-an hall. Later, he came down the path through a grove in the moonlight and returned to the Fuji Room of the Hōjō, or head priest's quarters. As the years passed, this tendency to combine Zen observances and amusement continued. The diary of a Shingon priest named Mansai (1378–1435), to cite another example, contains this entry:

> The weather is fine. Went to the Saihō-ji. In full color, the autumn foliage defies description. The abbot accompanied me, and younger priests guided us. After looking at all the halls and pavilions dotting the grounds, we rode in boats on the pond to our hearts' content.

On March 18, 1433 the Fushimi prince Sadafusa visited the Saihō-ji and made these comments in his diary:

> I was escorted throughout the temple. No words can describe the beauty of the scenery around the pond. Riding in a boat on the pond with the old abbot was extremely amusing. Then I burned incense in the Shitō-an and went to the hilltop Shukuen-tei to enjoy the view of the fields before us and the distant scenery. I was shown the whole temple and came to think that the Pond of the Seven Merits in Paradise must look like the garden of the Saihō-ji. Nothing could be more visually enriching.

As the tendency to emphasize the aesthetic value of the garden grew stronger, Zen priests themselves—who were expected to be proficient in Buddhist language and poetry—came to look on the Saihō-ji as a source of literary inspiration. On the last day of September 1400, a Saihō-ji priest named Chūi Kyūkei drew up the following list of poetic topics related to the temple and its gardens. The ten

Mooring stones in inlet off Golden Pond.

famous places are Mount Kōin, the Seita Forest, the Shumyō Gate, the Daiketsu Bridge, Kishō Gate, Yūkoku Villa, Nanaore Slope, Kyōen Valley, Shōnichi Mountain, and the Taikō Field. The ten topics related to the Golden Pond were Yōgō Rock, Hōshō Rock, Suichiku Island, Hakuō Island, the Suishō Pavilion, the Ruri Pavilion, the Shōnan Pavilion, the Tanhoku Pavilion, the stone called the Gōdō Boat, and the Yōgetsu Bridge. The ten poems on Mount Kōin include such topics as the Kōjō Gate, the Tsūshō Path, the Baifū House, the Shitō-an Hall, the Ryōga Cave, the Ryōen Water, the Kiun Cave, the Zazen Rock, the Kongō Platform, and the Shukuen Pavilion. Finally, the ten pine trees are the Machō, the Garyō, the Hakkaku, the Manju, the Kosan, the Eppō, the Chinzan, the Keikan, the Shiun, and the Bon'on.

Kyūkei's list shows again how Zen made no distinction between the sacred and the secular, in this case in the form of poetic literature dealing with actual physical things. The Buddha and all things are one, and the compilation of such a list, which seems to interpret the garden space as an organized aggregate of individual elements, resembles trying to prove the existence of the earth by listing all of the cities scattered over its surface.

The latter half of the fifteenth century saw the first of a series of disasters that spelled the end of the Saihō-ji garden in its original state. For eleven years, beginning in 1467, Kyoto was torn by power struggles known as the Ōnin War. On April 22, one of the warring factions set fire to the Saihō-ji and reduced it—all but the Shōnan-tei pavilion, which stood on an island in the pond—to ashes. This disaster was followed by repeated destructions and reconstructions. In 1485, the temple was destroyed by flood, and restored by the priest Rennyo of the temple Hongan-ji. In 1568, the mighty warlord Oda Nobunaga destroyed it again; on this occasion, workers from Tanba, Izumi, and Kawachi took part in the reconstruction. Between 1624 and 1644, the temple was seriously damaged

by flood, and repaired by contributions from the villages in Tanba and Yamashiro. In 1688, floods destroyed the pond garden, which was left unrepaired. With this, all trace of the garden as it had been in the fourteenth and fifteenth centuries was lost.

Zen as a religion was for centuries patronized largely by the warrior class and enjoyed very little wider popular support. As long as the warrior families who were its financial mainstays remained in power, all was well. When they suffered grave defeats or died out entirely, the temples they had maintained had nowhere else to turn; they lost their ancient position and all hope of regaining it. When the Fujiwara family fell, all the lands Fujiwara no Chikahide had bestowed on the Saihō-ji were taken away, and the temple's splendid garden became something to fantasize about only in fiction.

From the early seventeenth to the mid-nineteenth century, the Tokugawa shogunate ruled the country from Edo (present-day Tokyo); the emperor and his court were relegated to a dignified but powerless existence in Kyoto. In the middle of the nineteenth century, political power returned to the imperial court, but the fortunes of the Saihō-ji declined even further. It was allowed to go completely to ruin, and nature regained her own to create a new garden. In the damp climate of the Kyoto region, mosses thrive in shady places. Most of them cling close to the earth; others make a thicker undergrowth resembling clumps of beautiful cedar boughs. Mosses of this kind gradually came to cover much of the ground under the trees at the Saihō-ji. The priests did not want this to happen—for six hundred years, they had tried to preserve some semblance of the temple—but their work was in vain. By now, the mosses have had their velvety way, and most Japanese people today are more familiar with the name "Moss Temple" than with the name Musō Soseki gave the institution centuries ago.

*Many gardens in Japan today are forced to work
the tourist circuit and often end up playing to
uncaring crowds. But some gardens still hold true to
their first purpose: to celebrate nature and to offer a
space for man's creative work and relaxation. The
author here selects a few examples from his store of
memory and experience: the garden of Shinju-an, a Zen
temple in Kyoto, used for spiritual training; the lived-in
garden of a house in a small village; a tea-ceremony
garden that is a stage for ritual and refinement.*

GARDENS
AT
WORK

View from the main gate to the entryway. A straight line of cut flagstones leads the visitor past the Kuri, or general affairs building. The trees are all carefully trimmed and shaped.

Entryway Garden. From the straight flagstone path (behind the closed gate), the visitor confronts these large stepping stones arranged in the auspicious three-five-seven pattern. The contrast is startling and, in the Zen fashion, is meant to be.

"Juniper" Garden. The stepping stones lead directly to the front of the Hōjō, where the garden is almost entirely taken up by a large pruned pine tree, meant to represent a juniper tree in a Chinese story about the priest Bodhidharma.

Three-Five-Seven Garden. Around to the east is this delightful area of low stone groupings on a mossy ground. There used to be a view of Mount Hiei, but the space is now enclosed by buildings and foliage. The eaves of the Hōjō extend way out over the garden, while the veranda and open shutters help to bring the garden into the building.

Tea garden of the Teigyoku-ken. The path of stepping stones jogs back to the veranda of the Tsūsen-in, where guests wait to be called to the tea ceremony. The low entrance (*nijiriguchi*) to the tea room is at the far left.

Crossover corridor connecting the Hōjō and Tsūsen-in. This shows how well garden and architecture are integrated at Shinju-an. The stone basin is provided for purifying hands and mouth before proceeding to the tea-ceremony room, the Teigyoku-ken.

North garden of the Tsūsen-in. The path from the Teigyoku-ken branches off and skirts the side of the tea room to emerge in the back, where it opens up into a more expansive zone filled with large plantings and standard props like lanterns and basins. It is lovely and tranquil here, very different from the teasing mood of the "Juniper" garden in front.

RESIDENCES

Shibayama Residence. This home was built in 1908 in a style typical of that of the silkworm farmers of this area. The garden was completed in 1925. It contains a pond and huge stone groupings, but its most noteworthy feature is probably the even huger examples of topiary art: Chinese black pine, sweet osmanthus, cypress. (Gunma)

Fukui Residence. This is the home of a saké producer. Built in 1897 under the direction of Hayami Sōgyū, a tea master, the main garden uses full-bodied stepping stones set almost flush with the ground. Note the perfectly circular pivot stone, and the large stones left and right immediately adjacent to the veranda. (Shiga)

Fukui Residence. Round, low stones here provide a pleasing counterpoint to the lines of the walkway, which is suitably forceful and direct as it leads into a more expansive area. There is an echo here of the path from the main gate, shown in the color plates to the following chapter.

Taira Residence. The Taira family were rich landowners in the Hokuriku area on Japan's north coast. Their garden covers some 13,000 square meters. The photograph shows how the traditional Japanese house opens to the outside. At the same time, an area of earthen floor is created next to the veranda and bordered by a runway that can be fitted with panels to block out heavy snow and drifts. This is a feature of the architecture of this region. (Ishikawa)

Murosaki Residence. Designed by Sonoyama Shounen in 1978, this garden uses a large black pine and mountainous stones to create a powerful dry-landscape composition. This is rather monumental for the size of the site, and may have been prompted by the great wall and hulking landscape beyond. The room that looks out onto this garden is carpeted. (Shimane)

TEA GARDENS

Urasenke Tea School. This complex of gardens and tea pavilions was established in 1647 by Sen no Sō-tan, grandson of Sen no Rikyū, the great tea master. It was devastated by fire in the 1780s, and its current form dates from that time. The path leading to the entryway, shown here, and the many other garden elements employed at Urasenke and the neighboring tea school, Omotesenke, have had a tremendous influence on Japanese garden design. (Kyoto)

Omotesenke Tea School. This is the headquarters of another school of tea founded by a grandson of Rikyū, Sōsa. The tea garden is designed to be walked through, and is thus called a *roji*, or "dewy path." The visitor is expected to leave the outside world behind and let the journey through the garden refine his spirit in preparation for the ceremony of tea drinking. (Kyoto)

Mushanokōjisenke Tea School. Rikyū's grandson Sōshu founded his tea school at a slight distance from the other two. The photograph here of the roji leading to the Kankyū-an tea room shows how the tea garden was laid out to resemble a mountain path and then studded with various functional and decorative elements like lanterns, gates, and basins. The gate here is famous for its braided roof. (Kyoto)

Omotesenke Tea School. At the very rear of the estate is the Fushin-an, which is said to be modeled on a tea house founded by Rikyū himself. The present structure dates from 1923. The guest to the tea ceremony enters the tea house through the square opening behind the wooden shutter. Inside is a room only three tatami mats in size. The rough-hewn posts and mud walls are emblems of the determinedly rustic taste carefully fostered by the wealthy and powerful of the age.

Kōtō-in. The entrance (*nijiriguchi*) to a tea room is such that a guest must stoop to enter, an exercise in humility. Before doing so he rinses his hands and mouth at the stone basin. While the view here of the garden from inside the tea room is lovely, when the ceremony begins the wooden shutter will be closed. The primary function of the tea garden is as an approachway to the tea room (Kyoto).

Urasenke Tea School. This is the roji of the Yūin tea room. A straight pavement leads to a squared-off stone basin inscribed with Buddhist figures, more decorative than religious in intent. What is interesting here is the way the pattern of stones suddenly "scatters" as it leads away from the basin to the left. In the ritualized setting of the tea garden, such displays of "naturalness" are a kind of prop, just like the stone basin, crafted and calculated to human concerns.

SHINJU-AN:
A ZEN GARDEN

Large Zen Buddhist temples generally include a number of subtemples, called *tatchū*, where the principal figure enshrined is not the Buddha himself but some former abbot of the temple who has himself resided in the subtemple where he is revered. One such subtemple is the Shinju-an in the Zen temple Daitoku-ji in Kyoto. The priest who is honored there is Ikkyū Sōjun (1394–1481), the forty-eighth abbot of the Daitoku-ji. Ikkyū was a talented poet and painter and a descendant of the Fujiwara family, one of the most illustrious in Japanese history. His disciples did not leave their master's residence after his death but stayed on to convert it into what is now called the Shinju-an in 1491. Given the civil disorder and strife of the time, it is unlikely that this early subtemple made pretensions to great splendor.

Though most establishments of this kind have been turned into tourist attractions, a sign on the gate of the Shinju-an declares that it is not open to visitors. The current priest in charge, Yamada Sōbin, was born in 1919; he describes himself as merely the man who must guard the Shinju-an in today's world.

Accounts differ as to how this subtemple acquired its name, which means "pearl (*shinju*) hermitage (*an*)." A work called the *Kosonjuku goroku* traces it to the story of the dilapidated house of a Chinese Zen monk named Yangqi, who spent his life in ceaseless wandering and for whom Ikkyū had the utmost admiration. It is said that one cold winter night snow fell through the broken roof of Yangqi's house, sprinkling the floor with white flakes that gleamed like pearls in the moonlight when the sky later cleared. Ikkyū is thought to have left the usual paper filling out of the sliding door panels of the Kuri (kitchen and general affairs building) of his subtemple, to allow the cold wind to blow in as a reminder of this story; hence the name Shinju-an. Still another version holds that the pearly snow on the moss of the tea-ceremony pavilion Teigyoku-ken in the Shinju-an represents the combination of severity and beauty characterizing Zen discipline and training.

The main gate of Shinju-an.

Portrait of Ikkyū.

The temple comprises approximately 6,000 square meters of land, two gates, and nine wooden buildings; there are only two inhabitants—the head priest and a novice in his twenties. Two women come in during the day to help with the chores. A young female helper greeted me when I visited the Shinju-an one day in the fall.

Sitting and chatting with the head priest in a tatami-floored room, I heard the call of a shrike in the garden. This migratory bird ordinarily comes to Japan only in late autumn; on that day, the maples had not yet started turning red. I learned from the head priest, however, that this particular shrike had taken a liking to the Shinju-an garden and remained there all year round.

. The garden I beheld that day was no doubt a far cry from the one that had existed in 1491, when the Shinju-an was first established. It is impossible to imagine that in those times of war when the priests sought truth in lives of poverty, the present buildings and grounds could have been created. A book called the *Sōchō shuki* describes the Shinju-an as it was in September 1526 and observes that the buildings were only temporary. There was nothing in the garden except a ritual washing basin, a few stones, and plantings of plum, camellia, and low bamboo. The Shinju-an did not achieve its present form until peace had been restored to the land in the early part of the seventeenth century.

The layout of the subtemple is in three main zones. The first is the one more oriented to the outside, and includes the main gate; the Kuri (1609); the Hōjō, or head priest's quarters (1638); and the residential building called the Tsūsen-in (1638). The main gate faces west. The most important of these buildings is the head priest's residence, which consists of six rooms and plank-floored verandas on all four sides and is roofed with cypress-bark shingles; it is used on only the most dignified and solemn occasions. In the central room, the head priest conducts services every morning, reading passages from the sutras in front of a Buddhist shrine that houses a statue of Ikkyū. Other

periodic services conducted at the Shinju-an include those held to commemorate the day of Ikkyū's death, on October 21; Urabon services in memory of the spirits of the dead, from August 13 to 15; and New Year's services, held from the night of December 31 through January 15. The rooms are unheated even in bitter cold. A small number of believers attend these observances.

The garden extending along the south and east sides of the head priest's quarters has a ground cover of moss, a few pine trees, and a low hedge. The largest of the pine trees spreads its branches wide and low in front of a white clay wall. Though the present pine was planted in 1932, its predecessor was also large and broad; like the tree there now, it symbolized the whole of this simple garden space.

Though probably without special interest for the ordinary casual observer, this garden is a kind of *kōan*—a problematic question or paradox that Zen priests put to their trainees to help them achieve enlightenment. The pine tree is a reference to a story about the great Indian priest Bodhidharma, who traveled to China and introduced Zen there in the early part of the sixth century. A Chinese priest named Jiaozhou asked Bodhidharma the true meaning in his journey from South India to China, and the great priest replied: "The juniper tree in the front of the garden." The head priest's garden is meant to recall that exchange; the substitution of pine for juniper was necessary since the kind of juniper mentioned in the tale is native to China and Korea and does not grow in Japan. When I asked Sōbin Yamada to explain the story to me, however, I found his explanation too difficult to follow.

The narrow stretch of garden on the east is popularly known as the Three-Five-Seven Garden; it contains fifteen stones in five groups, and a small number of plantings: azaleas, cypress, and a plant called *mokkoku* (*Ternstroemia japonica*). Since three, five, and seven are considered numbers of good omen, the garden symbolizes hopes for the head priest's good fortune. On the outer edge of the garden strip are a low hedge and a clay wall. At present a

Daitoku-ji Precincts and Plan of Shinju-an

1. Ryōgen-in
2. Sanmon
3. Butsu-den
4. Hō-dō
5. Hōjō
6. Sangen-in
7. Zuihō-in
8. *Shinju-an*
9. Daisen-in
10. Hōshun-in
11. Jukō-in
12. Ryōshō-ji
13. Kōtō-in
14. Gyokurin-in
15. Ryōkō-in
16. Kohō-an

Kitaōji Street

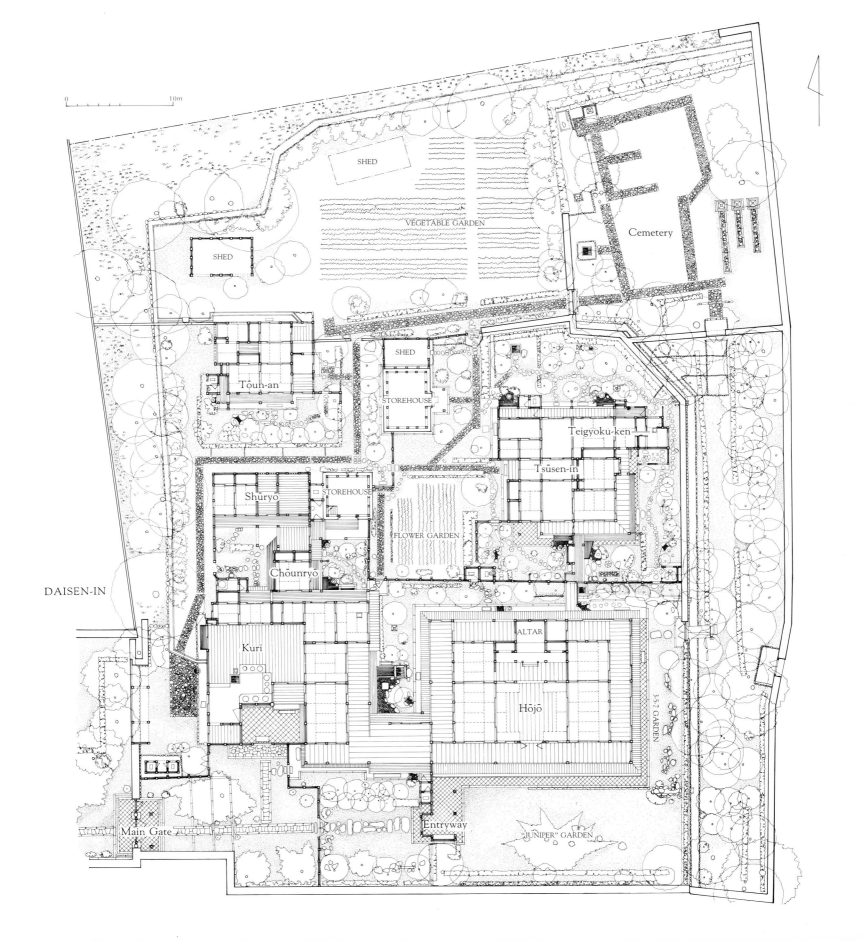

0   10m

SHED

VEGETABLE GARDEN

Cemetery

SHED

SHED

STOREHOUSE

Tōun-an

Teigyoku-ken

Tsūsen-in

Shuryo

STOREHOUSE

FLOWER GARDEN

Chōunryo

DAISEN-IN

Kuri

ALTAR

Hōjō

3-5-7 GARDEN

Main Gate

Entryway

"JUNIPER" GARDEN

stand of maple trees grows beyond the wall; in the past, before Kyoto grew to its present size, this garden commanded sweeping views of Mount Hiei and the rice fields on either side of the Kamo River. In other words, it was once an example of the kind of garden that "borrows" distant scenery for incorporation into its own design.

In contrast to the solemn south garden with its strong Zen philosophical associations, the east garden—adjacent to two rooms where the head priest receives his guests—is a place for relaxed enjoyment of the scenery.

The Kuri of a Zen temple is where food is prepared, records kept, materials stored, and other important day-to-day affairs conducted. The oldest building in the Shinju-an, the Kuri has an earthen-floored space (*doma*) with a well and a rice-cooking stove with nine compartments for firewood. Adjacent is a spacious, plank-floored kitchen/pantry; there are also rooms for temple administrative work, a twelve-tatami reception room for guests, a six-tatami room that corresponds to the living room of an ordinary house, and a four-and-one-half-tatami room where the head priest sleeps.

A garden surrounds the covered corridor connecting the head priest's quarters with the Kuri; in the center is a well. Once its water was essential to Buddhist ceremonies and daily chores; since modern plumbing was installed, the well has become largely a decorative accent. This attractive garden space can be admired from the reception and living rooms of the Kuri, from the head priest's quarters, and from the corridor.

The approach from the main gate to the Kuri, which is spread with white gravel and planted with trees, is also a simple kind of garden space. A guest proceeds past the Kuri along this approach garden to another inner gate, beyond which a path of large stepping stones leads to the entranceway of the head priest's quarters. Before this most dignified of all the Shinju-an buildings, the guest must compose himself and achieve a proper frame of mind; the garden is designed to assist him. The primary plantings are

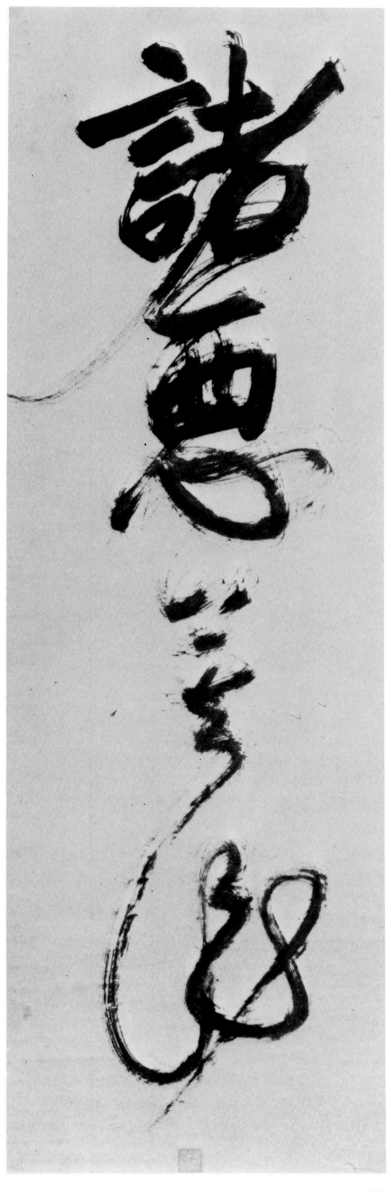

moss and trees, but the particularly large and unusually formed stepping stones are boldly set to startle in a way that seems consonant with the general taste of Zen priests. Immediately inside the gate is the south garden, where the visitor is confronted with the great pine tree and its puzzling reference to "the juniper tree in the front of the garden."

A single subtemple customarily has a number of residences for priests who are qualified for, but have not yet actually attained, the rank of head priest. The Shinju-an, for example, still has two such residences: the Tōun-an and the Tsūsen-in. In the past there were two others, the Tekitō-ken and the Umeya-ken, the names of which derived from Zen sayings. The *ume* of Umeya-en, for example, means "plum," and a Zen proverb observes that one cannot enjoy the glories of the plum trees in bloom without having suffered winter's bitter cold.

The Tsūsen-in, which consists of twelve rooms, was the dressing quarters of a grand lady in the court of the emperor Ōgimachi (1517–93). A court physician named Nakarai Zuisaku acquired it but, considering his own status too lowly to reside where personages of such high state had bestowed their presence, he donated it to the Shinju-an. Attached to it is a tea-ceremony pavilion called the Teigyoku-ken, designed in the style favored by the tea master Kanamori Sōwa (1584–1656). Thus while the Tsūsen-in is still called a residence, actually it is used today only for very special guests or as a place where those invited may wait to attend tea ceremonies held in the Teigyoku-ken.

The gardens of the head priest's quarters are designed to be looked at; the narrow space enclosed by the Tsūsen-in, the Teigyoku-ken, and the clay wall is designed as a tea garden—that is, to be walked through. It has stepping stones and strips of stone pavement; the guest who steps into the garden from the crossover corridor that connects the head priest's quarters to the Tsūsen-in finds a ritual stone water basin where he can purify his hands and

Teigyoku-ken interior.

Courtyard garden between the Hōjō and Kuri.

mouth, then walks along the stepping-stone path and turns left to the garden of the tea pavilion. Ordinarily, at about this spot would be a shelter where guests wait for their host to summon them to the ceremony. In this case, however, the veranda of the Tsūsen-in serves that function.

In the first division of the Shinju-an, then, all the open spaces between buildings and peripheral walls are treated in one way or another like gardens. All the buildings themselves are open and have surrounding plank-floored verandas; these function as neutral spaces, pivotal regions uniting the tatami-floored interiors with the gardens. When the rain doors and papered panels are pulled back, they are largely exposed to the outdoor air; in this sense the verandas are exterior spaces. On the other hand, they remain clean enough to walk on in bare feet, and are sheltered from rain and foul weather by deep projecting eaves; in that sense, they partake of the interior. Of course, these characteristics are by no means peculiar to the Shinju-an alone but belong to all traditional residential and Buddhist architecture. Nonetheless, openings and verandas must be taken into consideration if the way buildings and gardens are unified in traditional Japanese architecture is to be understood.

The second zone is much more private than the first. The main building has four rooms: three general living areas and one small room—three tatami mats with a storage cupboard—where the novice priest sleeps. In front of the room is a veranda 90 centimeters wide, and beyond that a tiny space that is a garden in name only. The novice and the head priest alike content themselves with very small living quarters because Zen philosophy teaches the virtue of poverty. The very act of tolerating life in cramped quarters is considered a spiritual discipline in itself.

To the north of this building is the residence called the Tōun-an, which is intended for priests qualified to have subtemples of their own. Since there is no one of that status in the Shinju-an at present, the building is empty. It

Vegetable garden behind Shinju-an.

has tea-ceremony-style garden spaces on the south and east sides. Two other residential buildings have been pulled down. Two ordinary clay-walled storehouses in traditional Japanese style protect the temple's valuable possessions and ceremonial furnishings.

Almost in the center of zones one and two, which are largely surrounded by clay walls or hedges, is a large flower bed; lovely in its own right, it is actually used to raise the flowers that decorate the temple altars and shrines. Indeed, in Japanese thought flower beds and flower gardens are not generally considered gardens at all. As if to indicate the flower bed's lowliness, all the surrounding buildings turn their backs or sides to it: on the southeast, on the other side of a wall, is the rear of the head priest's quarters; on the southwest, again over a wall, is the back of the Kuri; on the west is a wall and the long side of one of the storehouses; on the north is the long side of the other storehouse. Since it is not a garden the lovely plot of flowers finds no place in the more public first zone or even in the more private second one. It belongs instead to the third zone.

The innermost of all, this third zone includes the graves of generations of head priests and congregants, a fairly spacious vegetable garden, a shed for firewood, another shed for tools, and a windbreak forest and bamboo grove separating the Shinju-an from its neighbors. In this as in other Zen temples, tilling the fields, cleaning the graveyard, pruning the trees, and raking the fallen leaves are all aspects of spiritual discipline.

Yamada Sōbin is sensitive to the beauty of the place where he lives. "I am especially fond of the garden in two seasons," he says, "in May, when the vivid new leaves—so different in color from the green of midsummer—shimmer under a blue sky, and the white clouds float majestically by; and in the autumn, from the middle of November until early December, when the maples turn and the songs of birds intensify the silence."

But the garden is also a great deal of labor for the head

South garden of Tōun-an residence.

Shinju-an cemetery.

priest and his one novice; they and they alone are responsible for it almost all the year round. This is but one of many disciplines. At dawn they rise and prepare their morning meal; even eating demands a strict formal order. When this is finished, they begin cleaning the gardens. Their daily routine concentrates on the first zone only, and this takes the two of them about two hours. After a storm, it takes even longer. The novice takes care of the second and third zones alone, and looks after the vegetable garden when he finds time. Zen priests, of whatever age or rank, regard such manual chores as an aspect of their training equal in importance to reading the sutras and conducting services, or to study and seated meditation.

The one time that the novice and head priest are relieved of the garden chores is at the beginning of the hottest part of summer, when the trees attain their most vigorous growth. Then garden specialist Fujiwara Kanzō and some of his helpers come to do the heavy pruning. At this time only, as he sits on the veranda watching the gardeners trimming and cutting, the old priest seems liberated from his round of disciplines and duties. But, when the gardeners have gone home, he will have to clean up after them.

GARDEN OF A VILLAGE RESIDENCE

Almost all of the sixty houses in this small village are surrounded by hedges of Chinese black pine and have bamboo groves behind them. Crucian carp and other small fish dart about in the sparkling water of the stream that flows beside the narrow village road; the road is only wide enough to allow one automobile to pass at a time. In the past, landowners and tenant farmers comprised the bulk of the population; today, most of the villagers are employed in a town about 6 kilometers away and farm solely as a sideline. Even so, the houses retain the forms they had when agriculture was foremost.

The house under discussion here has a long gatehouse of the kind called *nagayamon* and a surrounding board fence. The pines, maples, and camphor trees rising above the fence indicated that this was once a landowner's residence. Postwar land reforms divested the owner of his holdings. Family elders died; children grew up and moved away to the cities. The oldest son has now retired from business and returned to the village to live in and look after the old house. Once a year brothers and sisters, bringing their families with them, return to conduct memorial services to their ancestors and to enliven the old building. The garden has not changed, but to understand the way the family originally used it we must travel back in time about half a century.

The plot of land attached to the house before World War II was the same size (5,000 square meters) as the site today; the accompanying plan shows only about one-third of the total. The remainder consisted of orchards and vegetable gardens exclusively for family use, an area for drying clothes, and a flower garden to supply the family Buddhist altar, the children's rooms, and the vases in the sitting and reception rooms. The plum trees that bloomed in early spring were planted for fruit. The irises in flower in early summer were intended to be used on the Boys' Day Festival on May 5. The zone was also planted with flowering peach, cherry, and quince and with many varieties of chrysanthemums, but this region is not shown

The entryway through the gatehouse.

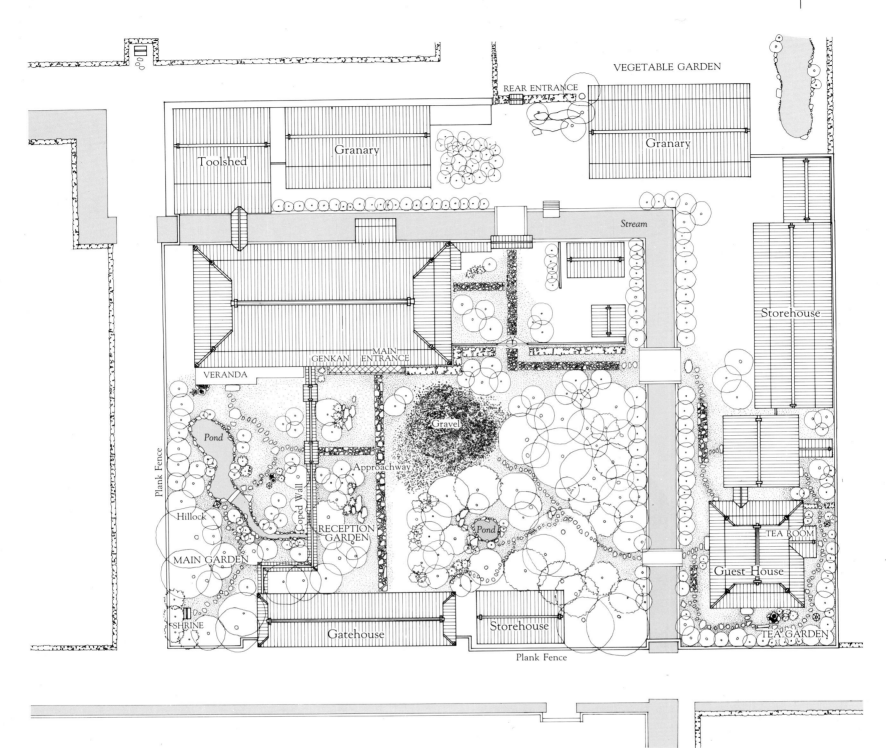

here because the family did not consider it a garden in the strict Japanese sense.

One of the major characteristics of the site is a stream that flows through it in an L-shape course. The bed of the stream, about knee-deep for an adult, is covered with pebbles. The stone dike is about the height of a child. The water is cool and clear. On hot summer days, children and adults alike could bathe and refresh themselves in it; in the days before the electric washing machine, women did their laundry here. One of the stream's greatest attractions, and a special treat for nighttime guests, was the darting of fireflies over its surface. When autumn breezes began to blow, crickets and bell bugs chirped in banks of bush clover whose blossoms reflected on the surface of the water. In winter, snow silently melted into the stream.

Another feature of the site is its three wells. Digging anywhere on this land yields abundant flows of fresh water; perhaps it would be more accurate to speak of three springs instead of three wells. One of them supplies

drinking water; the other two feed the garden ponds. The water seems warm in winter and cool in summer because its own temperature varies little. Modern plumbing has been installed in the village, but the people in this house prefer the well—interestingly enough, the waters are never muddied even after heavy rains. The plan of the garden is skillfully arranged to harmonize with the stream and wells.

In a modern middle-class Japanese home, the main garden space is intended for the family, not for the use of guests. This was not true in the Japan of the past, especially while the feudal system still obtained in society in general and in the family in particular: the garden was then primarily to entertain visitors. This is not to say that the family was entirely excluded from it. On ordinary occasions, they could also enjoy the main garden in their own way.

Inevitably, the form and style of the feudal-period garden reflected the social order, with the importance it gave to rank and position. Station was determined by the standing

The main garden.

of one's family. Human relations—with fellow villagers, relatives, co-workers, children's teachers, and so on—were important in maintaining the family's social position. It was important, therefore, to treat people of different ranks with due courtesy because to be remiss in this could have unpleasant results for the household.

Another factor, however, may have influenced Japanese ideas about the way to treat guests. From primitive times, folk belief has incorporated the idea of the "rare person" or *marebito*, the guest whose appearances are few and far between. No doubt this is intertwined in the popular mind with the ancient idea of *marebito* as gods from distant lands beyond the sea who appear on the rarest of occasions, bringing good fortune to this world and to the family they visit. Changing as it passed down from age to age, the idea of the *marebito* possibly has something to do with the care with which Japanese people treat their guests. This also explains the existence of the principal garden for guests in the southwest corner of this site.

Let us assume that a guest calls on the family on a spring day. Passing through the gatehouse, he proceeds directly along a stone pavement to the main entrance of the house. On his left are plum trees, *Ternstroemia japonica*, nandina, beech, and azaleas. In this zone, during the rainy season (June and July), seven peony plants grace the garden with countless blossoms. Small chrysanthemums carpet the area around an arrangement of stones. On the right is a small artificial hillock, a tiny pond with a spring, two varieties of fragrant olive, Chinese black pines, maples, sasanquas, and azaleas. Between the pond and the main house is a gravel-spread area large enough for an automobile to turn around in. A stone about human height and three pine trees screen the approach to the rear entrance of the house. At the boundary with the rear garden is a low hedge of Chinese black pine and a large oak.

Ordinary guests and members of the family come through the main entrance, which is fitted with three kinds of sliding doors: large wooden panels closed only at night,

shoji with wooden lower panels used only in the winter, and lattices used during the rest of the year. Though the lattice divides the inside from the outside, it has no key; anyone may open it. Part of the interior is visible through it from the outside; those inside can easily see guests coming through the gatehouse and walking along the approach garden.

A guest of higher rank than the family itself—the priest, for example, or the doctor—would not enter through this door but be shown to the more formal entranceway, or *genkan*, on the left. Even when the gatehouse is left open, the *genkan* is screened from view by the trees, stones, and peonies in the approach. When there are no guests, members of the family may sit and relax in the *genkan*, enjoying the cool southern breeze on hot summer nights.

The guest who enters at the *genkan* mounts two steps to an eight-mat tatami-floored room and turns left to enter the twelve-mat sitting room, with its ornamental alcove and set of staggered shelves; these two furnishings indicate that this is the most dignified room in the house. From here the guest has his first glimpse of the main garden, which may be made all the more beautiful if the host has watered the large footwear stone at the edge of the veranda and the stepping stones and trees in token of welcome.

The main garden is screened from the road on the side of the plot by a plank fence and from the approach by a plastered and coped wall. The wall has separate gates for guests and for the family and tradesmen.

The pond in the garden is surrounded by stone arrangements interspersed here and there with azaleas. Around the west end of the pond, where a spring constantly bubbles up, small pink flowers bloom in profusion in September to brighten gloomy rainy days. Beyond the pond is a small hillock planted with a dense grove of moss-covered trees, within which stands a small Shinto shrine. The path begins with the footwear stone at the veranda, passes by the spring in the pond and the guests' gate in the wall, and comes to a rustic earthen-

The bridge leading to the guest house.

The tea garden.

topped bridge, beyond which is the shrine with its stone lantern and ritual water basin.

Different elements play the leading role in the garden in different seasons. In early spring, when strong winds rustle the pine boughs, the plum and Japanese magnolia bloom. In early summer, the green of a huge maple overtops the roof to dominate the scene. In the early autumn, the *shū-kaidō* (*Malus halliana*) blooms; later, the maple and other deciduous trees assume their dazzling fall colors. In winter, snow obliterates everything in the garden but the black shape of the pond.

Guests enjoy looking at the pond from the reception room and never descend into or walk about in it. But when there are no guests, the parents are not averse to allowing the children to play there, chasing the carp in the ponds, darting among the trees to catch cicadas, or reading books in the shade. They are, however, strictly forbidden to climb the trees since this might spoil appearances by breaking branches.

Rooms to entertain guests in are on the south side of the main building. Those for the family—the dining room, kitchen, lavatories and toilets, sleeping quarters, dressing rooms, and maid's room—are on the north. On this side, the windows are all fitted with lattices, through which one may see a toolshed, two granaries, a general storehouse, and the gate leading to the vegetable plot in the rear. In a grove of trees beside that gate stand a persimmon and prickly ash, both of which are more practical than ornamental. The persimmon is there for its fruit; the prickly ash, for its tender young leaves and berries, used as spices and condiments. The tall rose mallows planted in profusion in this rear zone delight the eyes of the family at meals in late summer and autumn when they bloom with large, showy, pink and white flowers.

From a bridge crossing to the open space in front of one of the warehouses, one can look down at the stream or across to the patch of rose mallows, but the adults never take advantage of this prospect. The bridge is the domain

of the children, who sometimes dangle fishing lines into the water below, albeit with no intention to catch the fish—a kind of colorful carp called *senpara*—that swim to and fro in plain view. No one in the house (or in the entire village for that matter) would have eaten them. Buddhism forbade the killing of birds and fish, and *senpara* didn't taste very good. But the real reason is that these carp, all gaudy multicolors glittering beneath the surface of the water, are just too pretty. It was the family's wish that the stream be their sanctuary.

The third garden is on three sides (east, south, and west) of a separate two-story building in the southeast corner of the site. On the first floor are four tatami rooms; along the side of the main room, in the southwest corner, is a board-floor veranda 2 meters wide. When they are closed, the paper shoji panels become a screen on which flash shadows of swaying boughs and flitting birds. When they are open, the main room commands a view across the stream and through a grove of trees to the approach garden in front of the main house.

On the second floor are two tatami rooms; one is open on three sides and surrounded by a planked veranda with handrails. This vantage point looks out over the garden and across the rippling waters of flooded paddy fields to a range of blue mountains, snow-capped even in summer. Indeed, this view dictated the design of the room.

One of the four rooms on the first floor is outfitted for the tea ceremony, and the land on the south and east comprises a tea-ceremony garden complete with stepping stones, ritual wash basin, and stone lantern. Since 1925, however, only one guest has stayed in the building: one of the late owner's college friends who came to see the fireflies on the stream flowing through the site.

Consequently, the children had the guest house to themselves; they were free to choose the rooms they wanted and to enjoy the garden as they saw fit. In winter, they selected a small room that was easy to keep warm, but they preferred the open, spacious second-floor room as

View from the guest house.

a place to do their holiday school assignments in summer. Only one occupancy rule was enforced: a sickly child's bedding was always spread on the tatami in the twelve-mat room on the first floor, since this was more convenient for the visiting doctor and those responsible for looking after him.

Lying in that room all day, the invalid could tell the approximate time and imagine what was happening in the garden outside by the constant movement of gray shadows on the translucent paper of the shoji panels. In summer, for greater cool and comfort, the shoji are replaced with roll-up curtains made of the slenderest strips of bamboo. Through these one can actually see the garden; even better, as one sensitive young girl in the family wrote in her diary, one can imagine oneself in a setting out of the famous romance *The Tale of Genji*. This little diarist, who found her greatest joy in watching the changing moods of the garden from her sickbed, lived only a short time, a poignant reminder of how gardens watch over the people of a household and survive them for many years.

There are two ways to reach the main house from the guest house. One can cross the stone bridge immediately in front, follow the stepping stones through the dense grove of garden trees, and cross the open zone to the main entrance. Or one can take a more roundabout way, by ignoring the first stone bridge, walking along the shrubs by the stream to a second bridge, and crossing it to the east entrance. The first route cuts through the wooded part of the garden; the second skirts the garden entirely. At night, the more circuitous route was always chosen.

Walking on stepping stones, even on moonlit nights, is

difficult, but this was not the real reason. A paper lantern or a flashlight would have solved that problem. Children avoided the first route because at night the faintest breeze in the rustling leafy canopy of trees created shifting, menacing, black silhouettes.

The children ate dinner with the family in the main house. Later, they had to return to the guest house. The site was surrounded by a high fence, and there were locks on the doors, but the rain shutters were usually left open and the large window spaces characteristic of traditional Japanese residential architecture were filled with nothing but unlockable shoji panels. Any thief who wanted to break in would have had easy work with the guest house. In peace time, there was never an intrusion of any kind, but the children's mother always sent the maid to accompany them when they retired at night.

The maid would spread the bedding, lay out fresh clothes, collect the things to be laundered, and depart, usually with some comment or another. On one occasion, she said: "I'm always most afraid to go through the trees in the garden on nights when there's a crescent moon." Some days afterward, in the evening, as the family was eating dinner, an earthquake shook the house violently. For fear of another tremor, the father ordered everyone out into the grove of trees in the garden. Here he had deliberately set no stone lanterns or other objects likely to topple over, because he intended it as a place of shelter in emergencies. Later, when everything had finally calmed down and she was about to lead the children back to the guest house, the maid cleared her throat and said: "Didn't I tell you? Look, there's a crescent moon tonight!"

A TOWNHOUSE TEA-CEREMONY GARDEN

The tea room Shōka-dō in Kyoto. (From an Edo-period guidebook.)

Until the middle of the nineteenth century, this town was a thriving port, with a harbor well suited to docking and berthing sailing vessels. It was less satisfactory for steamships, however, and today the port has been filled in; public facilities, a thermal electrical generator plant, and housing developments have been built where ships once came and went.

The house I want to call your attention to is one I knew in my youth. In the age of sailing vessels it had been owned by a shipping agent. Located in the oldest part of town, it has been slightly remodeled but in general preserves the outer form it had when it was built in the eighteenth century. After World War II, an entrance and garage were added on the northwest, and the living room and kitchen were redone. The tea-ceremony room and garden, however, have remained virtually unchanged, except for the natural growth of trees and plants with the passing of time.

In the old days, most visitors came to the house on maritime business. The master of the household customarily entertained his guests with a tea ceremony before they turned to practical matters. When guests were few, the ceremony was held in the small (four and a half tatami) room; when there were too many people for this room, a larger (ten tatami) sitting room was used. This room could be further enlarged to nineteen tatami mats by removing the sliding partitions.

In keeping with classical compositional rules, the tea-ceremony garden is divided into an outer zone (soto-roji) and an inner zone (uchi-roji); the inner zone, however, is much longer and narrower than usual, and about three times the area. The location of the tea-ceremony room innermost on the site may have dictated this large inner zone; it may also have been the desire to enjoy views of the garden from the ten-mat sitting room when the partitions on its south side are pulled back. From there, a garden wall is visible beyond the plantings, and beyond the wall is the sea. In times gone by people may have sat in

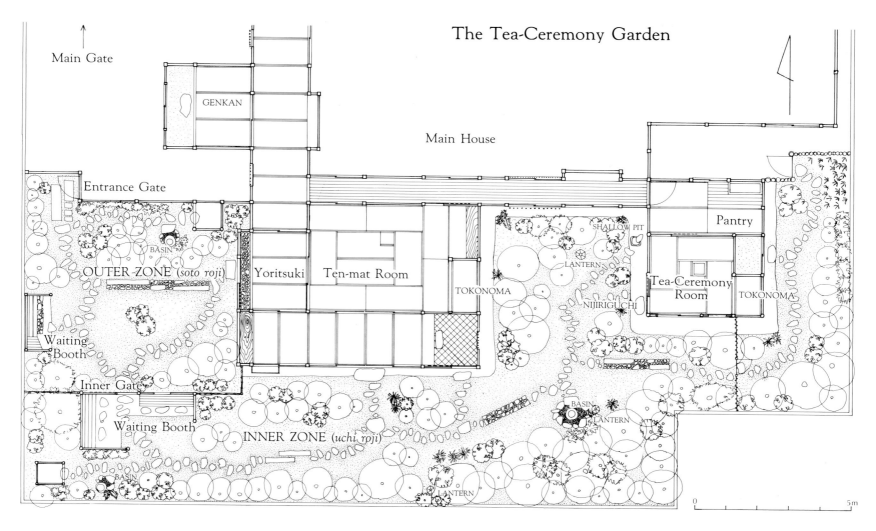

The Tea-Ceremony Garden

this room watching the ships about which they were negotiating going in and out of the harbor.

Though it may double as a pleasing prospect from the sitting room, this garden is designed fundamentally as a stage on which various phases of the tea ceremony are enacted. It cannot be seen from the tea-ceremony pavilion, the windows of which are to admit light but not to provide a view. Trees, plants, and stepping stones are part of the set. Ornamental in their own right, the water basins, stone lanterns, and waiting booths are also functionally essential.

We should recall that the tea ceremony demands as a setting more than a room in which to perform it and that the ritualized drinking of the tea itself is not its only event. While its purposes and rewards have changed with the passing years, for the last century the tea ceremony has been regarded as a way of cultivating etiquette and improving education. In the Momoyama period (1568—1615), warriors and merchants might gather to discuss the purchase of weapons over bowls of green tea. In a still earlier period, the beverage itself was regarded as medicinal; tasting and identifying the type of tea was a game and sometimes a form of gambling.

The nature of the ceremony as it is now practiced varies with the season and the time of the day. It is usually scheduled for noon, but can take place at other times. Dawn gatherings, held mostly in the winter, begin at four in the morning. In the summer, morning ceremonies may take place at six or seven. Some tea ceremonies are held at night. At ceremonies called *hango*, guests arrive after finishing their meal at home. Beginning around early December, special ceremonies are held to break the seals on jars of tea harvested that year. In the winter, the water for tea is heated in a sunken hearth called a *ro*; in the summer, it is prepared in a brazier and kettle called a *furo*. These variations—and changes of weather as well—make slightly different demands on the tea-ceremony garden.

Of all these different kinds of gatherings, the one that

impressed me most as a child took place at this house near the harbor at night, on the very last day of year 1931. In accordance with custom, water had been sprinkled on all the stones and plants in the garden, from the gate as far as the entrance to the tea house. In a staggered sequence on both sides of the pathway were ground lanterns with candles burning. Reflections of their light flickered on the damp earth and leaves. To me this was an all new, fantastical world—spread out before my eyes was a scene utterly different from the approachway and garden of the daylight hours. This must be a tea garden, my child's mind reasoned, something you see in the nighttime, and only on New Year's Eve.

If the truth be told, the tea ceremony that followed this vision was a most elegant affair, but I and my companion, the little girl in the family whose house we were visiting, were bored to tears by the adults' conversation. We had to be still and listen. After three and a half hours, the tea ceremony ended. We emerged into the tea garden. Now a soft snow was fluttering down, and the stepping stones and the moss and the tree branches were cloaked in a thin white powder. The ground lanterns had been snuffed out, but the light from the taller stone lanterns with their thick shielded mantles and from the waiting booth visible in the distance made the snow seem to blink and glisten, and yet another, more fantastical world unfolded before my eyes.

Taking this household as a model, let us look at a typical tea ceremony and in particular at the important role the garden plays in its enactment. In the standard ceremony held at noon, the host will ordinarily invite three guests, although under exceptional circumstances four or five—or as many as ten—may attend. Guests arrive between eleven and twelve. The host first serves them a meal (*kaiseki*) and then prepares two kinds of tea: *koicha*, a very thick brew made from the powdered young buds of old tea plants, and *usucha*, a much thinner drink made of ordinary powdered leaves. All preparations, including those of the garden, must have been completed well beforehand.

Preparing for a tea ceremony. (From a Meiji-period print.)

Nijiriguchi: the low entrance to a tea room.

Cleanliness is primary. The host rises early and cleans the tatami-floored reception room, the tea-ceremony room, and the garden itself, beginning at the entrance gate (roji-guchi). He cleans from the corners to the center and from above to below—that is, from tree branches to lower plants to the ground surface. Care is taken not to clean so meticulously as to alter natural appearances; the story cited earlier about the great tea master Sen no Rikyū shaking the boughs of the trees in his freshly swept garden, to create a more spontaneous setting, illustrates the approach the host must take.

When the cleaning is done, he washes down the trees and stones and, on three specified occasions, sprinkles the garden with water. He washes away any mud or dust clinging to scenic garden stones and stone lanterns, and cleans the compartments of the lanterns and the water receptacle in the ritual stone wash basin (tsukubai). Stepping stones are cleaned so that it is possible to walk barefoot on them—though no one will—without dirtying one's feet.

Next the host takes a damp cloth to the inner gate, the fences, and the seats, posts, and doors of the waiting booths and the tea-ceremony room. Of course, the wood will dry, but the wiping is timed so that it will still be slightly damp to give arriving guests an impression of cleanliness and beauty.

In the outer zone, near the waiting booth, and in the inner zone, near the low entrance (nijiriguchi) to the tea-ceremony room, is the chiriana, a shallow pit in the ground in which washed leaves and branches are placed to symbolize that the garden has been cleaned. The host must put fresh green bamboo trash-collecting chopsticks into these holes. He must then provide a new cryptomeria cedar dipper for the ritual basin where guests wash their hands and mouths. (The dipper used in washing the hands after a visit to the toilet is made of cypress.) His third task is to display the kinds of brooms used to clean the garden in strategic spots: beside the entrance to the tea-ceremony

room, in the waiting booth, or hung on a nail in the wall of the sand-toilet. Brooms for the outer garden are made from the leaves of a kind of palm (Trachycarpus excelsa); those for the inner garden are of bracken stalks. The brooms actually used are stored out of sight, and others of the same materials are displayed as if they had been used. Touches of illusion like this are frequent in the tea-ceremony garden.

Next the host must make things ready in the room called the yoritsuki: corresponding to the foyer of an ordinary house, this is where guests adjust their clothing, perhaps replace soiled tabi stockings with clean white ones, and generally prepare themselves for what follows. Shallow traylike boxes are provided for outer wraps and other accessories.

Before being summoned to the tea-ceremony room, all the guests come together in the outer waiting booth (machiai), where the host must now provide an array of things for their comfort: a box containing an ink stone, ink stick, and brushes; writing paper; powder for making an aromatic hot tea the guests may drink while waiting for the host to call them. In the corner farthest from where the principal guest will sit, he arranges a pile of small square cushions; on top of these, he places a tray containing implements for smoking.

To be strictly correct, the yoritsuki and the waiting booth should be separate, though they are often combined. If there is a tokonoma (ornamental alcove) in either one of these places, a scroll is hung there for the guests to examine. The host must select this scroll with care. It should not duplicate the theme of the scroll used in the tea-ceremony room itself, but should convey something of the nature of the implements and general mood of the gathering of the day; the scroll may be a painting or a work of calligraphy.

Sandals are set on the stepping stones in front of the waiting booth for walking through the garden. In the past, wooden clogs (geta) were used instead of sandals, but this

Chiriana: the shallow pit for holding garden "trash."

Machiai: the waiting booth.

practice has been discontinued since *geta* are more difficult to wear. On rainy or snowy days, large woven sedge hats are also provided, either on the seats in the booth or hanging from hooks on the wall. For cold weather, a brazier with live coals is placed in the booth. To take the chill off the water used in ritual purification, a bucket of hot water is set beside the basin.

The paths of stones in the garden may branch out right and left, making it difficult for the uninitiated guest to know which route to take. The host indicates the correct way by setting a fist-size stone tied in black bracken rope, called a *sekimori-ishi*, on top of the stepping stone that must be avoided. Sometimes a kind of tripod of green bamboo, called a *sekimori-dake*, tied together with black bracken rope, is used instead.

The three sprinklings of water cited above have important meanings of their own. If the area in front of the garden gate has been sprinkled, for example, guests know that the host has completed his preparations and they may enter; if it is dry, they understand that they must wait. Of course, it is rude to come late to a tea gathering and troublesome to the host to arrive too early: the custom is to arrive if possible fifteen minutes before the appointed hour.

Not just the area in front of the gate, but the entire garden must be sprinkled to create a distinctive freshness enhanced in the sunlight or the flickering illumination of lanterns. The performance of the so-called *sanro*, or "three dews," will differ according to the season, the weather, and the time of day.

Water is sprinkled generously in sunny places, but even more is called for in the shade to treat guests to the refreshing sight of drops falling among leaves. The mist rising from water evaporating in the sun, too, is considered attractive. The quantity of water sprinkled is greater in summer and on sunny days than in winter and on cloudy days. An especially plentiful drenching is given stones, trees, and ground for nighttime tea ceremonies, to reflect

the candlelight along the path.

The first of the three sprinklings—the "first dew" or the "water of greeting," as it is called—is performed after the garden has been cleaned, timed so that about one-third of it will have dried when the guests arrive. When they have entered and proceeded to the waiting booth, the host has a few more tasks to perform. He once again sweeps the tea-ceremony room and makes whatever adjustments are necessary to the fire, the implements, and the scroll hanging in the alcove. He burns incense in the charcoal over which the water for tea is being heated. Next he goes to the garden and with a dipper sprinkles water around the ritual stone basin. He rinses his own mouth, pours water from the bucket provided into the basin, puts the dipper in its correct position on the basin, and then replaces the bucket in the entrance to the pantry (*mizuya*).

Then, at last, he opens the inner gate to greet his guests for the first time. All bow silently to him. He returns the bow in the same silence, returns to the pantry, closes the door, and waits for his guests to enter the adjacent tea-ceremony room.

As soon as he is out of sight, all except the principal guest return to the waiting booth. The principal guest passes through the inner gate, rinses his hands and mouth at the ritual basin, and proceeds to the tea-ceremony room. The second guest follows suit, as do all the others. The last guest piles the cushions neatly in a corner of the bench in the waiting booth and closes the inner gate as he goes through. Inside, the guests admire the implements, scroll, and other appurtenances of the ceremony to follow.

Next the host serves his guests the *kaiseki* meal, which generally consists of soups, fish and vegetables, and saké and ends with hot water in a covered, spouted container. When this is brought in, the host returns to the garden for the second sprinkling. At the same time, he replenishes the water in the ritual basin. (There is obviously no need to sprinkle water on a rainy day; and no water is needed when the ground is covered with snow, which is

Tsukubai: the stone basin for washing before the tea ceremony.

Sekimori-ishi: the stone that bars the path.

considered lovely enough in itself.) He returns to the tea-ceremony room just as his guests finish eating.

At this point, the guests retire for a brief rest in the waiting booth in the inner garden. Meanwhile, the host removes the scroll from the alcove, replaces it with flowers, and prepares the room for the actual serving and drinking of tea. When all is ready, he sounds a gong to indicate that the guests may return. Before coming back in, they once again rinse hands and mouths at the basin. Inside, they again examine the implements on display. The two kinds of tea are now prepared and offered.

When the tea has been drunk, the host performs the third sprinkling, this time of the inner and outer gardens and the area in front of the main gate to make things fresh for his guests' departure. From beginning to end, the entire procedure usually takes four and a half hours.

It should be clear, then, that the tea-ceremony garden is less an object of contemplation or viewing than an integral part of the ceremony itself. It is designed, cleaned, and even watered in accordance with the special aesthetic dictates of that ceremony; the skill with which the owner plans and uses it for the pleasure of his guests is a matter of utmost importance. And clearly, holding a full-scale tea ceremony is a matter too complicated to be undertaken lightly.

The actual tea garden I have taken as a model for my discussion here is virtually unchanged today from what it was in the past. I was not invited again to a tea ceremony there after that snowy New Year's Eve in 1931. My father got sick and died the following year, and I left home to go

away to school. One early winter day in 1963, however, thirty-two years later, a single yellow iris wrapped in an elegantly folded white paper was delivered to my door. In Japan, while there are of course many different flowers, it is customary to offer not a bouquet but a single flower, to represent all the flowers in the world. The person who sent me this gift was the daughter of the owner of the tea garden, my companion three years older who, as a child, had suffered with me in silence the tedious conversation of adults, and shared with me that fantastical vision of the tea garden. She of course had used the traditional way of offering such a flower, and she had attached a card formally inviting me to a tea ceremony on the coming New Year's Eve. In a small hand she had added the note: "The branches of the nandin tree by the garden entryway are this year filled with small berries, red and ripe, just like long ago."

It was then I remembered. When, in the midst of the falling snow, we had said goodbye in the garden after the ceremony that night, there by the gate were branches of red berries, dusted with delicate white snowflakes. At most tea ceremonies, the general attitude of the tea connoisseur is expressed by the phrase, often repeated, *Ichigo ichie*—you perform each action with sincerity, as if you will never have the chance to do it again in your lifetime. Each tea ceremony is different. There is merit in this way of thinking. But there are things that can make even of the spirit of *Ichigo ichie* a single experience. Here, for me, it was the snow-covered red nandin berries by the tea-garden gate.

Gardens in the traditional style are still being built in Japan today, particularly in the smaller sites surrounding private homes, inns, and restaurants. Public areas and modern blockhouse structures demand a different treatment, and tastes today are both eclectic and determinedly forward-looking. Where will the new breed of designers go for inspiration, and what will their gardens look like?

THE MODERN JAPANESE GARDEN

Nakamura Residence. Architect Saitō Yutaka's 1979 design for the home of the potter Nakamura Kinpei puts an open courtyard garden into the middle of what is essentially a big concrete box. A traditional Japanese space creates elegance in a crowded modern city. Wall colorings inside and out are used here to particularly good effect. (Tokyo)

Ichitani Residence. In 1979 designer Kubo Tokuzō used large boulders to prevent this garden from being overwhelmed by a large hill that looms up directly behind. The effect is curiously light-hearted: are these hippos wallowing in a stream? The fence is part of the design, not a boundary marker. The shrubbery is trimmed to reveal the matching stone in the background. (Tottori)

Kasai Residence. Kubo Tokuzō enjoys using long stones in the shape of hexagonal prisms, although these are never seen in traditional Japanese gardens. Note, however, that if you were to draw only the outlines of the major stone configurations of this garden (1981), you would get the standard three-part stone grouping consisting of one vertical piece and two horizontal ones for balance. (Kyoto)

Inoue Residence. This minimalist courtyard garden was designed in 1972 by Fukaya Kōki. It uses low-lying cut stones, water, and a few plantings in what would otherwise be dead space. Perhaps the most interesting aspect of this garden is the way the water follows no particular stream bed but simply oozes across the stones. Randomness, in other words, is built into this modern garden. Traditional Japanese gardens celebrate organic processes by organizing them. (Tokyo)

Fukui Residence. See the color plates to the preceding chapter for more of this garden. Bending the path along the main entryway allows the gardener to block the visitor's line of sight and reveal a distant scene at just the right moment. It also makes a small space feel larger. The stone basin with standard lantern is probably here primarily for decoration. (Shiga)

Sono Residence. The various gardens for the Sono family's home were built in 1921 under the supervision of Seisai, the 12th-generation head of the Urasenke tea school. Here, in the courtyard garden, the fine stems and airy leaf patterns of the bamboo are used to offset the weight of the stones and basin, while the height of the plantings on the right gives the entire composition a rich balance. (Ishikawa)

Konnichi-an. Iwaki Sentarō was born in 1899 and studied under Ogawa Jihei. A student of tea, he has built many tea gardens; the garden here is part of the large traditional roji-style garden built for the Tokyo headquarters of the Urasenke tea school in 1957. Reed blinds are often used in the summer in Japan: they let in air while preserving the privacy of the home. (Tokyo)

Chōshō-an Tea House at the Ōkura Hotel. Typical themes of an outdoor tea garden—a stone basin and lantern—are evoked on the seventh-floor of a luxury-class hotel by designer Iwaki Sentarō (1955). The problem of how to care for plants and where to root them indoors has been handily solved here by leaving them out entirely. (Tokyo)

Kochō Restaurant. Believe it or not, this restaurant complex—150 square meters of trees, courtyard gardens, paths, and four separate pavilions—is on the sub-basement of a building not far from the crowded Ginza. The mood is one of perpetual twilight, although cherry, persimmon, citron, and other trees are brought in at appropriate times to "change" the seasons. Work was completed in 1969 after a design by Iwaki Sentarō. (Tokyo)

Ken Domon Museum of Photography. Various leading designers have contributed to the museum housing the work of one of Japan's great photographers, completed in 1983. Among these is Noguchi Isamu, the sculptor. Noguchi's garden uses an ascending-descending theme of concrete, steps, and water, accented by bamboo and an upright relic. (Yamagata)

Dokkyō Medical School Hospital. In 1976 Iwaki Sentarō designed this courtyard garden of boxwood hedge for an open-air space on the hospital's eighth floor. The checkerboard pattern is a standard motif. What is of interest here is how Iwaki adapted it using an irregular layout, deep gutters between the stones, and hedge blocks of varying sizes to give the space volume and texture. (Tochigi)

Konishi Shuzō Brewery. Fukaya Kōki has here (1974) made a garden of exceptional interest. The spread of water and the scattered setting of stones and moss (*Ophipogon japonicus var.*) create a primordial zone. But the stone basin from which liquid pours forth, though primitive, is elevated and ceremonial. It is possible to read some version of the creation myth into this garden, but the message may have more to do with the fact that Konishi, the owner, makes a beneficent saké. (Tokyo)

Kashima Construction Company, Akasaka Annex. This is a "roof" garden in a basement and was built by Iwaki Sentarō in 1964. Because of its site, Iwaki could only use small plantings, but he has arranged them and included a hillock so that there is a different view from every angle, including this one, looking down from the lobby on the first floor. New spaces, views, moods, and uses—these are a few of the challenges facing Japanese gardeners today. (Tokyo)

ASSIMILATION AND GROWTH

The Japanese people first encountered the idea of public parks in the latter half of the nineteenth century. When a band of isolationists set fire to the British legation in Gotenyama, a former mansion of the shogunal family and a popular recreation spot for viewing cherry trees, the Tōkaidō highway, and Edo (Tokyo) Bay in the distance, the anger that gave rise to the incident was explained as reaction against the construction of a foreign building in a place that one writer compared indirectly with London's Hyde Park.

Of course, parklike compounds where people could stroll and enjoy the scenery predate Gotenyama, but most of them were the compounds of large Buddhist temples or Shinto shrines. In 1868, however, when the reins of government passed from the Tokugawa shogunate to the imperial court, the new leadership was determined to catch up with the advanced nations of the West, and included in their program was the provision of parks. The government actually created nothing new, but simply designated as public parks the temple and shrine grounds that had served as recreational spaces in the days of the shogunate. This policy did not primarily represent a return of recreational land to the people or a desire for the restoration of natural scenery in the city; it was no more than one aspect of the government's modernization and Westernization program, and as such was seen by the general public as novel and strange.

Hibiya Park, the first Western-style park created in Japan, was planned by Honda Seiroku (1866–1952), a professor at the School of Agriculture of what was then Tokyo Imperial University. The park was not purely Western in style, however; 70 percent of the landscaping was Occidental, and 30 percent completely Japanese in tone. Nor was it in any real sense eclectic: the two parts did not meld but existed independently, side by side, an illustration of what I call the Japanese accretive approach to cultural borrowings. Other examples of this approach can be seen in private gardens as well, among them the Seibikan

Furukawa Garden Residence, Tokyo. Meiji period.

Yamato Bunka Museum, Nara. Garden by Yoshida Isoya, 1960.

Hiroshima Telecommunications Building. Garden by Fukaya Kōki, 1980.

Residence (Aomori Prefecture, 1909) and the Furukawa Residence (Tokyo, 1917). Josiah Conder (1852–1920), an Englishman invited to Japan to teach architecture at Tokyo Imperial University, included—no doubt at the client's request—Japanese elements in the garden he designed in 1913 for the Mitsui Club.

In other words, while they imported Western garden styles, the Japanese did not abandon their own traditions and felt no need to effect an eclectic blending of the two. When the Confucian Maebe Jūkō (1828–1908) designed Nara Park in 1894, for example, it was in a completely Japanese style, and contained no Western elements at all. Either ignoring or misunderstanding the philosophy on which Western gardens are based, the Japanese of those days cared little about the odd coexistence of new and old.

Scientific gardening methods came to Japan from the West by two academic routes: forestry and horticulture. Later the disciplines were to be embodied in mutually opposed organizations; the study of forestry gave birth to the Garden Society of Japan (Nihon Teien Kyōkai), and the study of horticulture to the Japanese Institute of Landscape Architecture (Nihon Zōen Gakkai). Working together, however, representatives of both fields planned the gardens of the Meiji Shrine in Tokyo, completing the Inner Garden in 1921 and the Outer Garden in 1926. They decided to make traditional Japanese garden ideas the keynote of the plan, even as they incorporated Western approaches to landscaping; thus a pond planted with irises became the central theme of the Inner Garden.

From about the middle of the nineteenth century, as modernization got underway, the numbers of traditional-style gardens constructed in Japan actually increased. The clients for whom they were built, however, were no longer the shogun, the feudal lords, and the court aristocracy but government officials, businessmen, and wealthy landowners. Typical of these were the gardens of villas built in the foothills of Higashiyama, in Kyoto, in the late nineteenth and early twentieth centuries. Conduits from Lake Biwa,

east of Higashiyama, intended mainly for use in generating electricity, supplied the water for these gardens, the earliest of which was the Murin-an, built in 1896 for the soldier-statesman Yamagata Aritomo (1838–1922) and still extant today. Yamagata's approach to the garden as an idealization of nature through "adjustments" and "corrections" was consonant with ancient Japanese ideas on the subject, but he refused to allow himself to be bound by Kyoto conventions and traditions. He, for example, did not hesitate to use fir trees—formerly considered unsuitable—for the grandeur they impart to the design and for the ease with which they can be raised to great sizes. Yamagata had the help of the gardener Ogawa Jihei (1860–1933), who participated in repair work on practically all the famous Kyoto gardens.

There are two ways of evaluating the mixture of old and new, East and West, in the gardens of this period. Positively speaking, it was an enriching diversification. Negatively speaking, it was a source of confusion in the Japanese cityscape.

Gardens in the past were confined to shrine or temple compounds and to private residences; architecture itself was—except for castles—limited to religious and residential styles. Tokugawa government offices were in Tokugawa mansions; schools were in Buddhist halls or residential buildings. As Japan modernized, however, many new and different kinds of buildings were needed: government buildings, schools, museums, hotels, railway stations, office buildings, factories, retail stores, and so on. All these different kinds of buildings required garden spaces, but for some time no attempt was made to have the garden conform to the nature of the building, or to develop new and original garden styles. The gardens of the Akasaka Detached Palace, for example—modeled on French palace architecture and currently used as the national guest house—are totally Western in style.

Imaginative garden designers for the new age were slow to emerge, but educators and public officials with some

Sakusetsu-ken, Akita. Garden by Iwaki Sentarō and Shirai Seiichi, 1970.

education in the modern science of landscaping were able to draw on people from other fields for garden work. Trained largely in the agriculture departments of colleges and universities that focused on forestry and horticulture, the gardeners themselves were understandably weak on the artistic side of their work. Furthermore, they were rarely called upon to design gardens in the Western style. The introduction of outside ideas compensated to some extent for these shortcomings.

The participation of outsiders in garden design had, in fact, already begun in the late nineteenth century. The designer of the above-mentioned French-style gardens for the Akasaka Detached Palace was Katayama Otokuma (1853–1917), an architect. Later, many other architects and artists turned their hands to garden design: Murano Tōgo did the gardens for the Kasuien Annex of the Kyoto Miyako Hotel (1960) and the Shigetsutei (1959); Yoshida Isoya did the garden for the Yamato Bunka Museum (1960); Tange Kenzō designed the garden for the Kagawa Prefectural Hall (1958); Horiguchi Sutemi did the Uraku Garden (1972). Nagare Masayuki and Seiji Shimizu are sculptors and have both designed gardens. So have Shigemori Mirei and his son Kanto, both garden historians. Iwaki Sentarō was a gardener. Fukaya Kōki, who has designed a number of modern-style gardens, never had any formal training. Garden builders Mori Osamu, Nakane Kinsaku, and Nakajima Takeshi all studied landscaping.

None of these people could work without the help of the old-fashioned gardener, the man who actually does the work and who knows what can and cannot be done in planting, stone arranging, pond planning, and other aspects of garden design. Gardeners have been important—if often anonymous—figures for centuries. Today architects, sculptors, and landscape designers need the cooperation of these men more than ever before.

People from other fields tend to regard work in the world of gardening as a realm for self-expression. The traditional garden was often a microcosm or idealization of nature that could easily lapse into conventionality and leave no room for creative thought. If it had symbolism of a kind, it lacked concepts of abstraction. Modern designers, however, especially those who come to the garden from other disciplines, demand more freedom and favor the abstract; in that regard they turn with particular eagerness to one older design tradition: the *kare sansui* gravel-and-stone garden. Avant-garde designers use split, crushed, and cut stones of kinds that are never employed in the traditional approach; good examples include the garden of the suburban office of the Hiroshima Telephone and Telegraph Public Corporation (1980), by Fukaya Kōki, and the rooftop garden of the Tokyo Tenrikyō Building (1962), by Nagare Masayuki.

Not only abstraction and the use of novel materials, but vastness of scale characterizes the Japanese garden of today. This development, which dates to the 1960s, was stimulated in part by the rapid growth of the Japanese economy and is exemplified by large parks and open-air museums: the Japanese Village Farmhouse Museum in Osaka (1960), Meiji Village Museum in Aichi (1965), Nopporo Forest Park in Hokkaido (1968), the National Kyūryō Sylvan Park in Saitama (1974), and National Shōwa Memorial Park—currently under construction in western Tokyo. These large-scale projects have only the most tenuous connections with the traditional, premodern Japanese garden.

This is not to say, however, that the old-fashioned garden has gone entirely out of fashion. Quite the contrary, gardens for strolling, gardens with ponds and streams, and stone-and-gravel gardens are still being made. It is not uncommon, moreover, to see the same designer who does creative modern work designing—once again, probably at the client's request—gardens in traditional and conventional styles.

Thus the cast of mind that, since at least the thirteenth century, has enabled the Japanese to adopt and adapt the

Sumiyoshi Shrine, Hyōgo. Garden by Shigemori Mirei, 1966.

new without abandoning the old still prevails. Gardens designed for a way of life four centuries old are still being created; ancient gardens are constantly being reconstructed; the popularization of the tea ceremony has resulted in the making of more tea-ceremony gardens than at any other time in history. At the same time, there is a continuous assimilation of forms and materials from the West. Japanese gardens still have distinctive characteristics of their own, but this is a period of groping in the dark, of repeated attempts to discover the forms of the future. The outcome of these efforts remains uncertain; but if past experience is a guide, as long as the industrious, knowledgeable, practical Japanese gardener continues to exist, he will work hand in hand with architects, sculptors, painters, ikebana teachers, tea masters, and amateur clients to evolve combinations of many elements—a creative process in which all are united and none is obscured or obliterated.

Over the years conventions have been established
regarding the use of various materials in the Japanese
garden. Streams are shallow and curving, stones are set
in odd-numbered groups, lanterns are located behind
stone basins or at a fork in a pathway. Most often
these practices follow from function, but sometimes it
is just a matter of historical precedent or everyone
agreeing that one style is somehow more appealing than
another. These shared notions about how things should
look are a principal design source at the basis of
every discussion between the owner of the site and the
person responsible for turning it into a garden.

ELEMENTS OF DESIGN

一 立石口傳

要旨

"Sakutei-ki" section dealing with stones and plantings.

THE MATERIALS
OF CREATION

At least as early as the Heian period (794–1181) there existed in Japan a group of painters called *niwa-eshi* who specialized in drawings of projected gardens. Sometimes they were the garden designers and creators themselves, doing this kind of work as a sideline; sometimes they were artists in their own right. The oldest record of garden paintings of this kind relates to the repair of the vast Toba Detached Palace in the southern part of Kyoto that the retired emperor Toba (1103–56) undertook in 1135. At that time, one Hōgen Seii of the Tokudaiji family presented Toba with a drawing of the pond in the garden as it would

look when completed. This same Hōgen Seii is known to have done repair work on the waterfall in the garden of the temple Hōkongō-in, which had been constructed in 1133 by a stone-setting priest named Rinken. No doubt, gardeners of the period were also expected to be good with pencil and brush.

These garden paintings, however, could not have been functional specifications and designs. While it has always been possible to make a drawing of a completed garden, in Japan a design revealing what a proposed garden will look like when it is finished is impossible because

Ginkaku-ji, Kyoto. (From an Edo-period guidebook.)

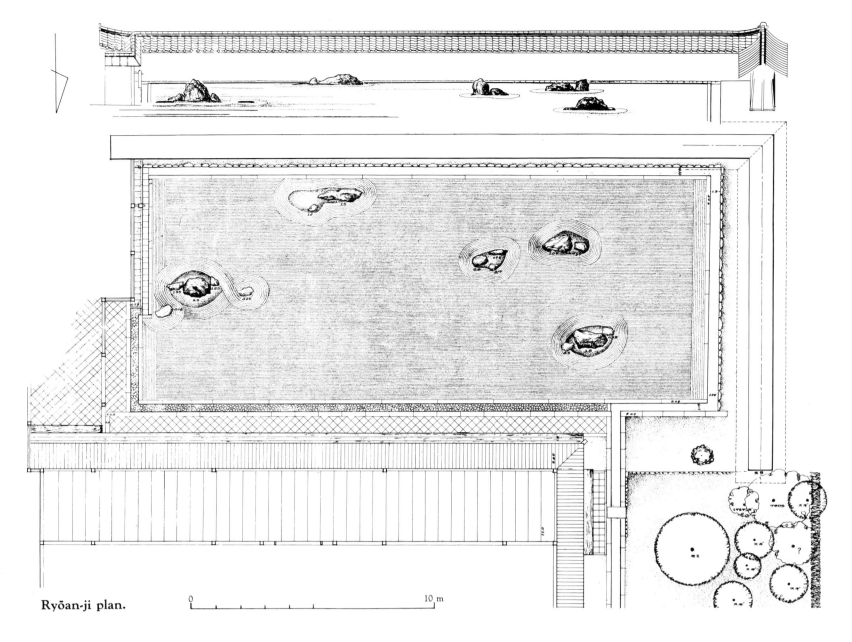

Ryōan-ji plan.

0   10 m

the designer cannot accurately foretell what shapes the natural stones and plants he must use will take. One can depict a pond of such-and-such a shape in a given location, a waterfall tumbling from a certain mountain, a stream flowing in a certain direction, deciduous trees in one area and evergreens in another, or iris-and-stone arrangements in the pond. Apart from such artificial elements as stone lanterns and basins, however, the forms and sizes in a Japanese garden are naturally determined and therefore different in each case. Garden paintings were for the most part made merely to satisfy the wishes of the owner.

In recent times, clients are especially eager to know what their gardens will look like before they are constructed. In the hope of obtaining commissions, garden designers comply with the wishes of clients, though they are fully aware that a truly accurate forecast is beyond their powers. Fortunately, garden projects do not require local government permits and are not subject to the regulations that govern architectural construction. The designer, who has a general knowledge of what kinds of stones are to be had and what kinds of trees and plants are on the market, can proceed from very general plans of composition, conferring with his client on changes that may be necessary as work progresses.

The client exerts considerable influence on the garden designer since he probably has his own ideas about the kind of garden he wants; he is also paying the bills. At the same time, the designer has his own preferences, knows what is technically possible and impossible, and has an idea of what results the decisions made now will have far in the future. Given the nature of gardening materials, the conflicts that are likely to arise between client and designer

mean that mutual trust, cooperation, and the patient evolution of ideas are essential. It is virtually impossible for a stubborn individualist to produce a Japanese-style garden entirely on his own.

It is because this system prevails that the creator of the famous Murin-an villa garden in Kyoto (1896) is sometimes said to have been the gardener Ogawa Jihei and sometimes the owner, the high government official Yamagata Aritomo. In the traditional Japanese system, the making of a garden has never been left entirely to a professional gardener; the process of creation has never required a landscape artist in the Western sense, because the work has always been a cooperative effort.

An attitude of humility and profound respect for their materials—and their clients—has always guided the men who create gardens. The famous garden of the temple Ryōan-ji, in the western part of Kyoto, consists of a moderately small plot of land spread with white gravel and set with fifteen stones of various sizes. Because Japanese gardens often strive to re-create natural settings or to symbolize the teachings of Buddhism, Taoism, or Confucianism, there are many different interpretations of the Ryōan-ji garden. Some people see it as a vision of the sea, dotted with small islands. Others think it represents a tiger leading her cubs. People today tend to disregard such interpretations and find it more convincing to see the garden as an abstract composition. One of the fifteen stones in the garden is important in connection with this discussion, since it bears on its underside an inscription of two names. One of them is Kotarō; the other is so worn away as to be illegible. One Japanese novelist has suggested that gardeners of the despised *kawaramono* class carved

Hōshun-in garden, Kyoto.

Natural stone near Nara, with images of sun and moon made by anonymous carver.

their names on these stones to assert their pride in having created the Ryōan-ji garden. But the assertion is groundless: even today, in circumstances much more liberal than those prevailing when the garden was produced, garden designers do not carve memorials to themselves in lasting stone.

A Kyoto gardener acquaintance of mine, Okuda Masatomo, expressed the following opinion of the novelist's idea: "That stone is one of the boundary markers that still turn up from time to time in the mountains around here. That's why it has two names carved on it. Someone picked it up and brought it in from the mountains. Garden stones are not modern sculpture. We don't sign them. If we did, the garden owner wouldn't like it."

Okuda's comment underscores two important points. First, the social standing of the gardener has traditionally been too low for him to assert himself by signing his work. Second, natural stones are works of art produced by the slow hand of nature and are not to be tampered with by man. Kotarō and his anonymous neighbor, who put their names on a boundary stone to settle a property dispute, would no doubt find the novelist's attempt to add something new to the Ryōan-ji tradition wryly amusing and might even go so far as to comment on the powerful imaginations of people who lack actual knowledge.

STONE GATHERING

Very few Japanese gardens fail to include natural stones in one way or another. The garden of the Shōden-ji, in western Kyoto, uses only raked gravel and pruned azaleas; but the plants are employed as if they were stones. The garden of Chinese bell flowers at the Hōshun-in abbot's residence, and the maple garden of the Kōtō-in abbot's residence, both in the compound of the temple Daitoku-ji, might seem at first to have no formal stonework; but it is there nonetheless, arranged unobtrusively to simulate the appearance stone would have in a natural setting of field and mountain.

The importance of stones is further emphasized by the fact that garden designers were called "stone-setting priests" from as early as the twelfth century. Ancient primitive beliefs asserted that divine spirits reside in stones; while these beliefs died out long ago, they may still have something to do with the conviction that stones are not proper objects for man's creative interference, but natural works of art in themselves.

Apart from transport costs, the prices of natural stones—which are displayed in dealers' lots in the casual way they occur in nature—have no set standards. A stone found on a hill, in a stream, or by the sea has no value whatsoever to someone who considers it a kind of natural jetsam. The same stone, however, may be prized to the extreme by another person who sees within its crannies some fathomless beauty. A kind of granite called Kurama stone, from the Kurama region near Kyoto, is considered expensive. One way of accounting for this high cost is the elegant brown color produced on the surfaces of the granite by the oxidation of its high iron content; another is that Kurama stone is in such limited supply now that it is officially forbidden to remove any more of it from the region. People who are unattracted by the rust-brown color of course have no interest in Kurama stone.

Garden stones come from no special locales. They are found in mountains and valleys, in marshes and river beds, by the seashore, sometimes on road construction or riparian work sites, and sometimes in other people's gardens that for one reason or another must be destroyed. Dealers buy such stones; if no agreement on price can be reached, the stones are simply buried in the ground. For the sake of convenience, however, since stones from similar locales have certain characteristics in common, garden materials are classified as mountain stones, lowland stones, river stones, and seacoast stones.

I recall walking along the banks of the Hozu River in the mountains north of Kyoto and coming upon a band of men who struck me as odd because of the sharply

Hideyoshi at Daigo, March 15, 1598. (From a Momoyama-period screen painting.)

contrasting ways they were dressed. Some wore the garments of laborers; some were dressed like craftsmen and skilled workers; and one appeared to be a person of means who might have employed the others, though he did not seem to be supervising the party at the time. When I asked one of the men what they were doing, he replied, "Looking for stones to use in gardens." I was startled at this since the Hozu is under government control, and I assumed official permission was required for the removal of stones from the banks and riverbed. As a matter of fact, I was correct.

Stones are prized for two reasons: their associations with the past and their appearance of great age. One example of the former is the Fujito stone, which was found on Fujito Beach in Kurashiki, in what is now Okayama Prefecture. In either the late fifteenth or early sixteenth century, it was carried by ship 180 kilometers and then hauled overland in a two-wheeled cart another 50 kilometers to be set in the garden of the home of the Hosokawa family—high officials in the Muromachi shogunate and military rulers of Awa province in Shikoku.

In 1569, the warlord Oda Nobunaga (1534–82), who began the process of unifying a war-torn Japan, started building a new mansion in Kyoto for the shogun Ashikaga Yoshiaki. On March 3, the Festival of Peach Blossoms (or Girls' Day as it is now called), to the accompaniment of flutes and drums of all sizes, he led from three to four thousand workers who hauled the Fujito stone, covered in rich brocade and floral decorations, from the Hosokawa house to the new mansion, where it was to be installed in the garden. The parade was a demonstration of respect for the shogun on the part of a conquering country warlord, but it is interesting that this stone was considered valuable enough to serve as the focus of that demonstration.

By 1586, the shogun Yoshiaki had been banished and the mansion destroyed. A new military ruler, Toyotomi Hideyoshi (1536-98), was in power and decided to build for himself a residence called the Jurakudai. The Fujito stone

became one of the ornaments in the garden of the Jurakudai, but it was not to remain there long. On March 15, 1598, five months before his death, Hideyoshi held a sumptuous flower-viewing party southeast of Kyoto at Daigo and stayed in the abbot's residence at the temple Kongōrin-in, now called the Sanpō-in. There he had extensive renovations made to the grounds, apparently in preparation for another flower-viewing party to be held the following year for the emperor Goyōzei (1571–1617). As part of the project, the Fujito stone was moved to the garden of the Sanpō-in, where it remains today, richly endowed with the kinds of historical associations that make it priceless. The almost monstrous shape of this stone may have appealed to the tastes of warriors who lived in a time of turmoil but, frankly, fails to please me.

The second major determinant of the value of a stone is the appearance of age. Since World War II, stones split at the quarry into interesting and accidental shapes have come to be admired and used in many new gardens— including some as notable as Tange Kenzō's garden in 1958 for the Kagawa Prefectural Hall. Traditionally, however, Japanese garden designers have avoided freshly quarried stones in favor of those that, through years of exposure to wind and weather, have developed a distinctive natural patina.

This patina of age, called sabi, differs with the provenance of the stones: there are mountain patinas, sea patinas, and patinas unique to stones that have aged in gardens. Of course, the virtue of the patina is in the eyes of the beholder: some people find supremely satisfying a look of antiquity that others condemn as dirty and unsightly. There are even dealers who treat stones with chemicals and bury them in the earth to develop the appearance of a natural patina specifically for those who appreciate it.

Some stones, however, no matter how old, are considered to be in bad taste; their grotesque forms, for example, put volcanic rocks into this category. They are

Fujito stone at Sanpō-in, Kyoto.

rare in gardens; and, when they do occur, it is generally as an outlet for the owner's frustrations. Some perhaps overly distinctive stones are prized for their textures, especially when wet. One such is a large greenish blue stone from Kishū, in Wakayama Prefecture, in the stone-and-gravel east garden of the Daisen-in abbot's residence of the Daitoku-ji temple. On the green-blue ground of the stone appear white stripes that evoke the foaming cascade of a mountain waterfall. Similar greenish blue stones, which may come from Shima, in Mie Prefecture, and Iyo, in Ehime Prefecture, as well as from Kishū, are in the Sanpō-in garden, in the second compound of the Nijō Castle, and in the garden of the Nishi Hongan-ji temple, all in Kyoto.

Although the concentration of famous gardens in that area makes Kyoto the center of most discussions of garden stones, other regions have suitable kinds of their own; the variety is virtually limitless. As natural works of art, it makes no difference where they come from, but it is customary to speak of "local" stones and "traveler" stones; the fifteen stones in the Ryōan-ji garden are a mixture of local varieties and those brought from elsewhere.

STONE STRUCTURES

Though natural stones come in many shapes, for the sake of convenience gardeners designate six faces, like those of a cube, and give each face a name. The front side is called the *mitsuki* (sometimes pronounced *mitsuke*), which may be vertical but is more likely to slant right or left, forward, or to the back. The right and left sides are called *mikomi* and like the front may slant or have irregular planes. They usually do not form right angles with the front. The top surface of the stone is called the *tenba*.

Unlike many stones in nature, garden stones are always partly buried in the ground. The submerged part is called the *shiki*, and the line at which the stone disappears into the ground is called the *ne* (root) or sometimes the *suso* (hemline). Obviously, the depth to which the stone is buried determines the form of the *ne*. Gardeners pay the

Dry waterfall at Daisen-in, Kyoto.

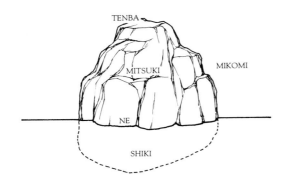

Parts of a stone.

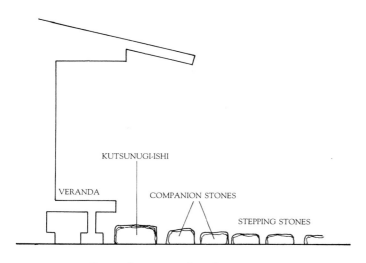

Stone for removing footwear.

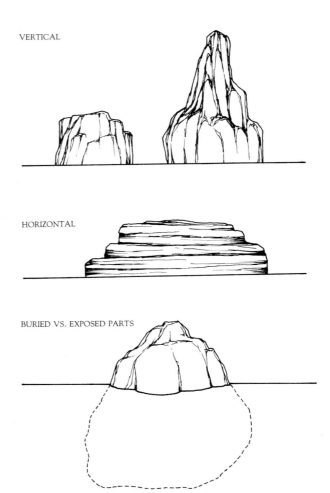

Decorative stones.

greatest attention to both depth and line since these factors have an important influence on the beauty of the stone and its appearance of stability.

Let us consider briefly at this point the locations and uses of stones in traditional Japanese gardens.

(1) *Kutsunugi-ishi*, or the stone on which visitors remove their footwear. This stone is placed at the edge of the veranda; because of the function it serves, it must be flat on top. Sometimes perfectly flat natural stones are available; sometimes, stones are trimmed and made rectangular. The eaves of traditional houses are deep, and the *kutsunugi-ishi* is set well under them so that when it rains it is possible to remove one's footwear without the protection of an umbrella and still remain dry.

The two stones immediately adjacent are considered to form a group with the footwear stone, distinct from the stepping stones of the path from the building into the garden. The heights of these two stones are carefully graded to effect a transition from the large footwear stone to the lower stepping stones. The harmony of the three elements of the group is an important consideration.

(2) *Keiseki*, or decorative stones. These are usually set singly to complement areas of lawn or moss or the approach to the garden. When there is no stone sufficiently attractive to serve this purpose alone, two stones—one smaller than the other—may be combined. And when even this does not meet the need, low plants may be added.

In setting these stones to best advantage, there are three major considerations. First, some stones appear more harmonious and attractive set vertically (*tate-ishi*) and others suggest a horizontal orientation (*yoko-ishi*). Stones that are relatively thin and have a large top surface (*hira-ishi*), for example, lend themselves readily to horizontal setting.

The second concern is to set the stones so that to the viewer's eye and imagination they seem as large as possible. One might assume that exposing them to the maximum extent would be the best way to achieve this effect, but

such is not necessarily the case. Presenting a stone to full view often gives an impression of lightness and smallness, whereas burying a large part of it creates the illusion of an immense boulder rising from the earth. It is said that, in Kyoto gardens, 90 percent of some of the stones is concealed underground; I suspect that from 50 to 70 percent is closer to actual fact.

The third concern is the position of the decorative stone in relation to the rest of the garden. A stone may sometimes give the impression of casual placement but can be set in such a way as to become a focal point of attention and a vital element in the total composition.

(3) *Ishi-gumi*, or stone groupings. A group of three or more stones combined in a complete aesthetic form is called an *ishi-gumi* (sometimes *iwa-gumi*). Primitive religious belief held that stones are dwelling places of divine spirits, and sacred stone groups are still to be seen in the compounds of Shinto shrines. But as this belief declined, attention turned toward the actual stone groupings themselves and to their aesthetic appeal—as representations of mountains, valleys, and riverbeds or, in modern years, as abstract art.

Stone groupings are often the basic frame elements of a garden since they are the only elements that can be expected to last for a long time. Because of these associations with the ageless and eternal, client and gardener used to conduct a ceremony whenever one was brought to the garden site.

Now, of course, trucks and cranes make the transport and setting of even large garden stones a relatively simple matter, but such was not the case some fifty years ago in Kyoto. In those days, a cart drawn by three oxen was required to haul a stone into town from a valley in the mountains in the north. It might take a whole day or even two or three to move the stone from its original location to the road and onto the cart. Once the stone was loaded, the drovers would wait till night to set out, perhaps because in some distant past it was felt that sacrosanct

Stone-hauling procession for Tokugawa Ieyasu's castle in Shizuoka. (From an Edo-period screen painting.)

stones should not be exposed to view until they were in their destined positions. Perhaps the practice had something to do with the primitive belief that spirits are on the move late at night, but the custom was no doubt observed without conscious knowledge of its origins. The purely practical concern for pedestrian safety in the narrow streets may also have played a part.

The cart would reach the client's house, if it was in the central part of the city, before dawn. The master and mistress of the house, the grandparents and sometimes the children, would be up and waiting. At the gate would be a paper lantern decorated with the family crest, serving as both illumination and a votive offering to the stone that was about to arrive. When the cart finally did appear the family held a small party with saké and food for the gardener and his laborers and with water, fodder, and a rub-down for the oxen.

The party was more than a mere formality. It symbolized the determination of client and gardener to cooperate in making the finest garden they could. The exchange of drinks was a sign of agreement; no contracts were ever drawn up to seal it. Mutual trust was the basis for such undertakings; the client and the gardener—whose social standing was generally the lower—agreed to work together as equals.

Natural cliffs and crags at Rikuchū National Park, Iwate.

STONE GROUPINGS

The original design sources of garden stone groupings are natural settings: mountain boulders and cliffs; unusual groupings of stones in the beds of mountain rivers; stones along the banks of streams flowing through open plains; the sand, gravel, and green pines of beaches; the mighty boulders dashed by sea waves. Painters have long favored such scenes in their works; with their powers of observation and their ability to transcend nature in aesthetic representation, they have been employed as garden designers from ancient times.

According to a thirteenth-century document called the

Detail of "Kasuga gongen reigen-ki" scroll: the residence of Taira no Toshimori.

Shugai-shō, for example, at the end of the ninth century a court painter named Kose no Kanaoka was made supervisor of the gardens at an imperial residence called the Shinsen-en, which consisted of a vast spring-fed lake and groves for hunting. Kanaoka was especially talented in the landscape style known as *yamato-e*, which in his day was gaining ascendancy. In contrast to *kara-e*, or Chinese-style painting, *yamato-e* was largely indigenous in style, dealt entirely with Japanese subject matter, and was better suited to serve as a source of inspiration for garden design since it concentrated on landscapes and treated human figures as of secondary importance.

Kanaoka's great-grandson, Kose no Hirotaka (999–1003), was a painter of portraits and Buddhist devotional images but is also known to have covered some of the imperial palace walls with murals and was connected with garden design as well. The ancient classic on gardening, *Sakutei-ki*, quotes Hirotaka as having said: "Garden stones must not be set in desolate places. If any one of the taboos related to stone setting is violated, the master of the house will suffer misfortune, and his family line will not endure long." The book then gives a list of seventeen such taboos.

A contemporary of Hirotaka named En'en lived at the temple Anrakuritsu-in on Mount Hiei, where he painted Buddhist pictures in the *yamato-e* style; he is known to have done garden design as well. The author of the *Sakutei-ki* says that he was an orthodox follower of the stone-setting tradition and mentions owning one of his books. The scroll called the *Kasuga-gongen Reigen-ki* (1309), now in the possession of the imperial family, includes a picture of the mansion of Taira no Toshimori; it is a classical example of the kind of painting that served as source material for garden designers like En'en. The scene is a pond where water fowl play around a boat. On the shore are stone groupings, pine trees, and flowering and other ornamental plants. Pheasants grace a low, manmade hillock; rabbits play in a field covered with grasses and other plants; a stream meanders through the landscape.

In the fifteenth and sixteenth centuries, too, a small number of painters continued to practice garden design. Sesshū Tōyō (1420–1506), one of the foremost among them, based his style on Chinese ink paintings of the Song dynasty; his highly individual stone gardens put to practice the precepts of a style that discovers five distinct colors in the gradations of monochrome black ink. The garden of the Jōei-ji temple in Yamaguchi Prefecture, composed of stones, a pond and lawn, and pruned plants against a backdrop of mountain forest, is an example of Sesshū's work—a strongly Japanized version of a Chinese tradition.

Ink-painting traditions continued to influence Japanese gardens as late as the seventeenth century and beyond. The Chinese classic on painting known in the West as the *Mustard Seed Garden Manual of Painting* (*Jieziyuan huachuan*), for example, by the painter Wang Gai (1663–1712), was reprinted in Japan; it contains general rules of painting and illustrations of trees, mountains, human figures, and stones. Although the book was intended to offer models of brushwork, the pictures in it—especially those of stone shapes—became models for Japanese garden design.

As we have noted, stone groupings begin with combinations of two: a major stone and a smaller one that emphasizes the larger or compensates for whatever deficiencies it may have. The combination of the two is regarded as a unit, rather than in terms of component elements.

The fundamental arrangement, however, is of three stones representing the triad of heaven, earth, and man—which in turn is a symbol of the whole universe. The largest stone stands for heaven, the smallest for man, and the one intermediate for earth. Though interpretations differ, harmony is generally prized in such arrangements. Garden designers describe as a "smash" (*warete-iru*) a group in as harmonious a balance as possible. When four or more stones are combined, neighboring stones are thought of as one to the extent necessary to preserve the triad. Probably

Sesshū's garden at Jōei-ji, Yamaguchi.

"Autumn Landscape," by Sesshū.

the Japanese insist on this idea of the triad because they want the entire garden as well as each of its parts to represent a microcosm of the universe.

Since the middle of the nineteenth century, stone arrangements have been composed in accordance with abstract aesthetic principles, but this was not true in the past. We have already mentioned the seventeen taboos in the *Sakutei-ki*; until recently, these taboos—many of which smack strongly of magic—were invariably observed. To convey their general nature, I shall summarize a few of them here.

1. If a stone that is naturally vertical in orientation is used in a horizontal orientation in the garden, it will inevitably be possessed by a spirit and cause a curse.
2. No stone more than 5 *shaku* (about 1.5 meters) in height may be set east-northeast since it will then become the demon that enters from the unlucky northeast direction.
3. If a stone higher than the level of the veranda floor is set near the house, misfortunes will follow one upon another, and the master of the house will not abide there long. This restriction does not apply to Buddhist temples or Shinto shrines.
4. Setting a stone adjacent to the southwest post of the house will cause illness in the family.
5. If a horizontally oriented stone is set facing northwest, wealth will not accumulate in the storehouse. (Warehouses for valuables were often built in the northwest, the direction of wealth.)

Most of these "taboos," of course, indicate aesthetic or hygienic considerations prompted by Japan's particular climatic and ecological circumstances. Designers and clients observed them as aspects of garden know-how, but probably did not respond to them as prohibitions in the strict sense.

Detail from Chinese "Mustard Seed Garden Manual of Painting."

Tea garden designed by Iwaki Sentarō for his own Tokyo residence.

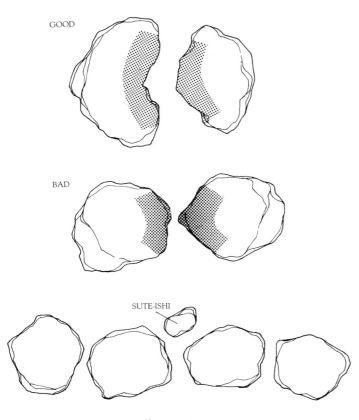

"Joining" stepping stones.

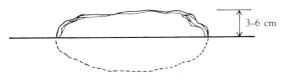

Setting stepping stones.

STEPPING STONES

I have already commented on the dual function of stepping stones—the practical and the ornamental—and on the different degrees of importance individual tea masters have given to each function. From at least as early as the beginning of the seventeenth century, paths of stepping stones have served as guides from the entrance to the tea garden, to the small inner gate, the waiting booth, the toilet, the ritual wash basin, the gate dividing the inner and outer tea gardens, and finally to the entrance to the tea-ceremony pavilion itself; the path is an important element in traditional Japanese gardens. The stones are generally of two sizes: those 40 to 60 centimeters in diameter, approximately big enough for one human foot; and those roughly twice that size, big enough to accommodate both feet at once. Paths consist mostly of one-foot stones, set at intervals of about 10 centimeters and interspersed with larger stones to heighten the decorative appeal of the arrangement. In other words, the standard is to set from four to five stones in a space of about 2 meters. The intervals accord with the gait of people dressed in kimono, and is somewhat shorter than the natural gait of people in Western-style clothing.

The natural stones used for these paths come in all shapes; it is the task of the gardener to set them in such a way as to generate a sense of harmony and continuity. This demands careful consideration of the contours of the stones—especially the shapes of the sides (*aiba*) that will be adjacent to each other. Since it is not always possible to obtain stones that can be harmoniously combined, sometimes small stones (called *sute-ishi* or "throw-away stones") are used to provide continuity between the stepping stones themselves. No one walks on these small stones.

No set rule governs how much difference there must be between ground level and the upper surface of the stone; this is also a matter of personal preference, but the standard is from 3 to 6 centimeters. A harmonious

Stepping stones in "flight of geese" configuration.

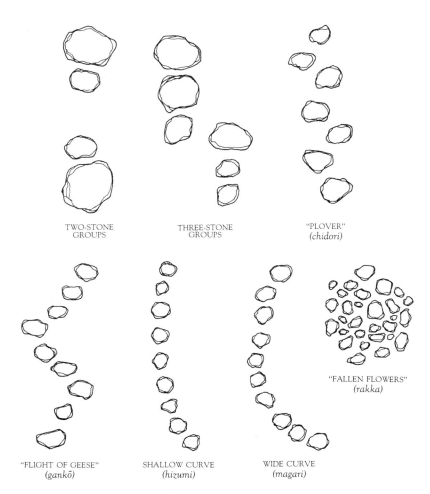

TWO-STONE GROUPS   THREE-STONE GROUPS   "PLOVER" (chidori)

"FALLEN FLOWERS" (rakka)

"FLIGHT OF GEESE" (gankō)   SHALLOW CURVE (hizumi)   WIDE CURVE (magari)

Path configurations.

appearance is easier to achieve if the stones are set high in small gardens and low in more spacious compositions. As is only sensible, the stones are set higher when the ground is covered with moss or lawn or when the garden is in a region where snowfall is heavy. In tea-ceremony gardens, the stepping stones near the tea pavilion itself are set lower and closer together than all the others, to inspire the visitor to walk more slowly and thus to become calmer and more composed for the events to come.

In laying out a stepping-stone path, it would seem enough to start at one end of the garden and end at the other. Because natural stones come in no definite, reliable sizes and shapes, however, this is not the case. To solve the problem and achieve the desired results, certain important stones—which might be called trump stones—are set first: the stones at the beginning and end of the garden; the stone where footwear is removed; the stone on which one stands to kindle a light in the stone lantern: a stone large enough for two people at the ritual water basin (the higher type of basin is called a *chōzubachi*, and the lower a *tsukubai*); the stones before and inside the inner gate; broad stones at pondside where people may pause to admire the scenery; and several others. The rest of the stepping stones are then filled in, but even this method does not ensure a harmonious arrangement at first trial. Often stones are put in place, found wanting, and then replaced with others that match better. Consequently, it is necessary to have on hand as large a number of stones in as many sizes and shapes as possible to choose from. The rejected stones are either buried or sunk in the pond; one garden designer has even remarked on the mood and appearance of stones visible through the water on the bottom.

Sometimes groups of large and small stones are combined to perform the function that under ordinary circumstances is served by one stone alone. These may be groups of two or three, and in any combination of large and small shapes. Sometimes a so-called group of five is used; considered to be sets of two and three, in combination,

such groupings actually consist of only four stones, one of which is counted twice as a member of both sets. Binding two groups of things together in this way by providing them with a common element occurs in other aspects of Japanese graphic and sculptural art.

Stepping stones virtually never form straight lines, which are considered hard to set, difficult to walk on, and unattractive. Instead they may be set in wide curves (*magari*), shallow curves (*hizumi*), or two kinds of zigzag lines: when each stone is set out of line with the next, the line is called *chidori*, or "plover," for its resemblance to the tracks this bird leaves on the beach; when each segment of the zigzag consists of several stones set in a straight line, the line is called *gankō*, or "flight of geese," as it recalls the V-formations in which these birds fly. In certain very special circumstances, stepping stones are set to look as if they had been casually scattered about. This setting is called *rakka*, or "fallen flowers." It should be noticed that, as in most other aspects of Japanese garden design, the stepping-stone patterns are modeled on real phenomena in nature.

GRAVEL PATTERNS

For the decorative ground patterns in Japanese gardens, sea or river sand has too fine a grain. It is readily scattered by the wind, and patterns raked into it crumble easily. Weathered granite gravel with a grain of about 5 millimeters in diameter is preferred; in Kyoto, the abundant gravel of the Shirakawa district serves this purpose in almost every garden.

We have already noted that in ancient times gravel was spread in certain areas as a symbol of religious purity. In the Muromachi period (1333–1568), it was used as a symbol for water in the gravel-and-stone gardens of the kind called *kare sansui*. One example of this is the garden of the Kitayama Residence, now called the Rokuon-ji or Kinkaku-ji (the Temple of the Golden Pavilion), built by the Ashikaga shogun Yoshimitsu. According to a book called

THE MATERIALS OF CREATION / 181

Raked gravel "waves" at Ginkaku-ji, Kyoto.

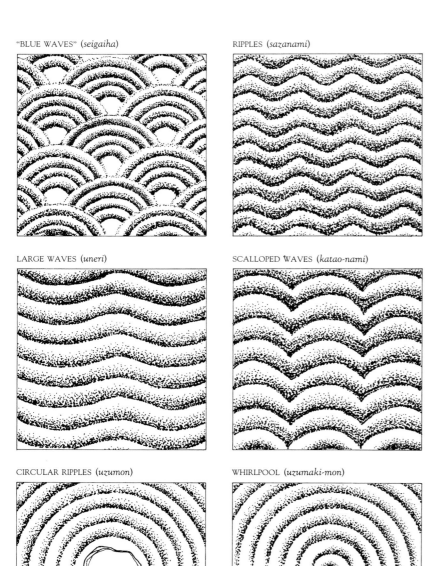

"BLUE WAVES" (*seigaiha*)

RIPPLES (*sazanami*)

LARGE WAVES (*uneri*)

SCALLOPED WAVES (*katao-nami*)

CIRCULAR RIPPLES (*uzumon*)

WHIRLPOOL (*uzumaki-mon*)

Gravel patterns.

the *Ashikaga chiran-ki*, the north and west of the famous gilded pavilion used on imperial visits were planted with early-blooming cherry trees, and between the trees and the building was a bed of gravel in five colors, raked into a pattern intended to represent wavelets on the surface of the sea.

Most *kare sansui* gardens were built in the precincts of Zen temples or subtemples, and sweeping decorative patterns in the gravel was one form of spiritual discipline. The usual patterns include ripples (*sazanami*); large waves (*uneri*); a scalloped wave pattern (*katao-nami*), mentioned often in Japanese verse; parallel zigzag lines (*ajiro-nami*); a pattern called "blue waves" (*seigaiha*), which resembles fish scales and is used in large gardens; a whirlpool pattern (*uzumaki-mon*); a circular ripple pattern (*uzumon*), used around stones; the so-called "lion" pattern (*shishi*); a whorling stream pattern (*kanzesui*); and combinations of these and many others.

STONE LANTERNS

Though some are in wood or metal, the overwhelming majority of garden lanterns are made of stone—most of them of a granite that has weathered slightly to produce the prized appearance of sobriety, age, and refinement. Granite is preferred also for the relative ease with which it can be worked.

Stone lanterns were originally votive lamps in front of the halls of Buddhist temples. In about the thirteenth century, they began serving a similar function in the precincts of Shinto shrines as well. Then, in the sixteenth century, tea masters began using them in their gardens; when this happened, stone lanterns of different and more creative original forms began to be produced for general garden use. No longer associated with religion, stone lanterns now serve as scenic attractions by day and for mood-making illumination by night, when oil lamps are set in their compartments.

Garden lanterns belong to one of three general styles.

Stone lanterns at Kasuga Shrine, Nara.

The oldest is the Taima-ji style, named for the temple of that name and dating from the eighth century. These lanterns are about 2.2 meters tall and consist of six parts: pedestal, shaft, middle platform, light compartment, roof, and jewel finial. Most of the lanterns in the Kasuga Shrine in Nara are of this kind.

The second style is that of the Korean temple light, which combines the roof and the jewel finial; it has a very large middle platform and light compartment and a short shaft, giving it a somewhat squat appearance. Since these lanterns are very big, they are at home only in spacious gardens; smaller modified versions have been worked out for more general use.

The third style is the creative, generating a variety of shapes unlike anything found in Buddhist temples or Shinto shrines. Representative of these are the yukimi ("snow-viewing") and Oribe lanterns. The former has a large roof and stands firmly on four legs; the latter is abbreviated in form and, lacking a pedestal, rises directly out of the earth. There is nothing to prove the assertion that the Oribe lantern style was originated by the samurai tea master Furuta Oribe (1544-1615). Some people call these lanterns Christian on the assumption—probably only a folk tradition—that the relief figures sometimes found on their shafts represent the Virgin Mary. This is unlikely since Oribe-style lanterns are found in the compound of the Shinto Kitano Shrine in Kyoto.

Since they do not provide very bright light, from the practical standpoint stone lanterns serve more as signs and as objects of admiration. But positioning them must take into consideration both practicality and beauty when they are used near the inner gate, the waiting booth, and the ritual basin in tea-ceremony gardens, in dark groves, or by the ponds of ordinary gardens. Since it is felt that the light in the lantern must be conspicuous to be worth appreciating, it is made brighter on moonlit nights than when the moon is not visible.

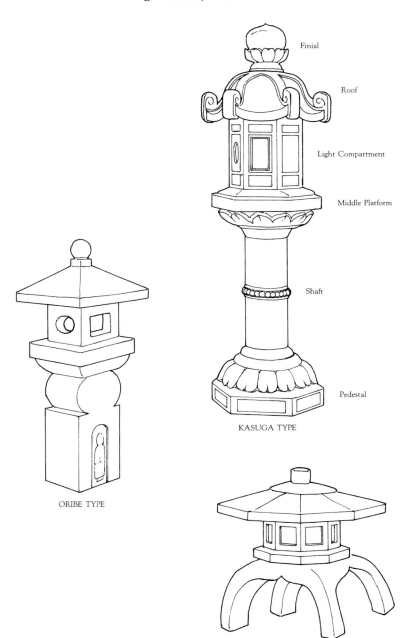

Stone lanterns.

雲
林
院
花
見

Heian courtiers viewing cherry blossoms at Unrin-in, Kyoto. (From an Edo-period guidebook.)

Sumiyoshi pine at Katsura Detached Palace, Kyoto.

PLANTS

Traditionally, plants for garden use are divided into two categories: garden plants (*niwaki*) and miscellaneous plants (*zōki*). *Niwaki* are almost exclusively those trees native to the secondary forests—the primary forests having disappeared millennia ago—in the vicinity of Kyoto, the center of most Japanese garden development. In garden use since at least the eighth century, these plants include pine, cryptomeria cedar, Japanese cypress (*hinoki* and *sawara*), Chinese black pine, gold-leaf plant, *Torreya nucifera*, *Pieris japonica*, pomegranate, crepe myrtle, *arakashi* oak (*Quercus glauca*), ilex, box, *Ternstroemia gymnanthera*, maple, camellia, cherry, Japanese magnolia, azaleas, and *Enkianthus perulatus*. The plum was an exotic introduced into Japan from China in the Nara period (646–794). Native to Japan and considered the abode of a divine spirit, the cherry was brought from the mountains into the city for the beauty of its flowers.

All plants not in this group were considered miscellaneous. Among these were the zelkova, which grows in eastern and northern Honshu; the fir trees, *Hamamelis japonica*, *Quercus acutissima*, and yew of cold climates; and the cycad of tropical regions. Originally scorned for use in traditional Kyoto gardens, these plants are found there now, though they are still regarded pejoratively as miscellaneous. In 1896, Yamagata Aritomo built his villa Murin-an in Kyoto and instructed his gardener Ogawa Jihei to plant fir trees in the garden. This was the first recorded use of firs in a Kyoto garden, but they have since been introduced from time to time. The numerous fir trees on the grounds of the Shugakuin Detached Palace were not there when the villa was first built, but date to repairs in the late nineteenth century.

Plants exhibit different qualities. The following are some of the points for which certain garden plants are prized.

1. Trunk. The form, color, or gloss of the stalks, trunks, and branches of certain plants, most of

Noh stage with painted pine.

Detail of "Maple-viewing at Takao," by Kanō Hideyori (ca. 1540).

them deciduous. *Torreya nucifera*, Chinese parasol tree, Japanese magnolia, plum, crepe myrtle, old pines, and so on.

2. Leaves or needles. The glossy leaves or needles of some plants, primarily evergreens. *Ternstroemia gymnanthera*, fragrant olive, and herbaceous peony.

3. Flowers. Particularly the cherry and the azalea.

4. Berries and fruit. Chinese quince, heath rose, *Melia azedarach*, nandin, and spear plant.

5. Autumn foliage. The maples, and sometimes the wax tree. (Because of salt winds, however, these are often less attractive in coastal regions than they are inland.)

Japanese gardens are condensed idealizations, but trees grow and must be tended if the landscape design is to be preserved. Pruning keeps growth under control. Pines are the most difficult trees to prune; this may be done by hand or with shears but is never mechanized, and is consequently expensive. In Kyoto, the prevailing method of pruning pines is to pluck by hand (*te-mushiri*) the maximum number of needles so that distant scenes may be viewed through the boughs. In Osaka and Tokyo, however, strong winds and sea breezes would blow away the remainder if the needles were plucked to this extent; shears are used instead to shape the trees (*hasami-sukashi*), and no thought is taken of distant views.

The most popular of all Japanese garden trees, in ancient times the pine was considered the abode of divine spirits. The customary painting of a pine on the wall behind the Noh stage recalls the belief that the drama itself was performed in honor of the divinity of that tree. Similarly, the Japanese people place pine-bough decorations in their doorways at New Year as an expression of the belief that the god of that festive and important season takes up residence in the tree. Apart from these associations, however, the pine is popular for its longevity, and the ease

with which it can be transplanted and trained into interesting shapes.

MOSS AND LAWN

Areas that are not planted with trees, spread with gravel, or occupied by a body of water may be covered with either moss or lawn. The Kyoto climate is so favorable to mosses that, without having to be planted, they often cover very wide expanses of gardens. This does not occur in Tokyo.

In Kyoto, the moss that appears naturally and covers most of the ground is short and green; the variety called *sugigoke* (*Polytrichum juniperinum*) must be planted, but is greatly prized for its longer, velvety growth. The abundance of this kind of moss at the Saihō-ji accounts for the popular name "Moss Temple."

Moss grows well under trees, in shady, damp places, in soil that drains well. The traditional way of preparing the soil for moss is to make a layer of gravel about 6 millimeters thick, top this with coarse red soil, and on top of this add a layer of a kind of clay plentiful in the Kyoto region. The moss is planted in the clay. Fertilizers will cause green moss to turn red and wither. In recent years, river water polluted with agricultural chemicals and domestic wastes shorten the life of mosses in some areas, while ordinary tap water usually contains purifying chemicals that spoil their colors. Mosses prefer natural underground water; to provide it some people have actually sunk wells solely for watering their moss gardens. Walking on moss crushes it so badly that it is unlikely to recover.

Lawn became a popular groundcover in the seventeenth century in connection with the stroll garden. Unlike many Western-style grasses that stay green the year round and require cutting, Japanese grasses are usually green only in spring and summer and turn beige with cold in winter. They do not grow enough to require mowing. The most familiar variety grows on embankments in the country and is called *noshiba* (field grass); because it takes firm root, this grass—which turns a beautiful gold color in the fall—is

Stream at Sengen-en, Kagoshima.

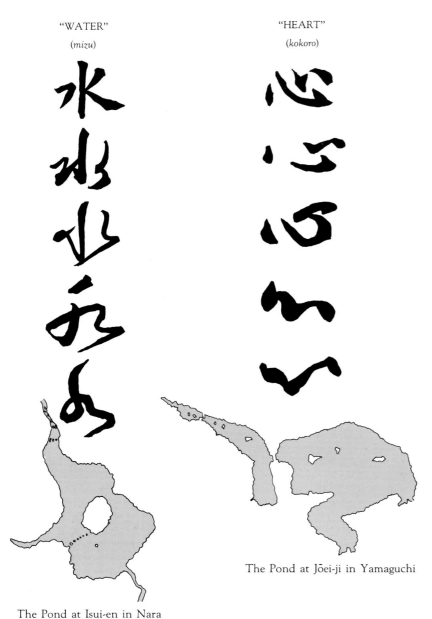

The Pond at Jōei-ji in Yamaguchi

The Pond at Isui-en in Nara

Pond shapes based on written characters.

often used to reinforce pond banks. In more recent years another kind of grass called Korean lawn (Kōrai-shiba) has become popular. Though it roots less well and is less attractive than noshiba, it is easier to grow and care for.

PONDS AND STREAMS

The shape of the pond is a matter of personal preference, though geometric forms are virtually never used. Ponds are modeled instead on natural bodies of water, shorelines, or Chinese written characters. Because these ideograms play so important a part in their written language, the Japanese have traditionally been accustomed to thinking of words as things more to be seen than heard: this has probably inspired the use of cursive forms of certain characters— particularly those for "mind," "river", and "water"—as pond shapes.

The custom of using the earth excavated in making a pond to erect an artificial hillock led to the evolution of a kind of garden called tsukiyama sensui, composed of such a hill and a pond fed either by a spring or by tapping a nearby source. Gardeners must take great pains to dig the pond so that it will look as large as possible when it has filled. Naturally, steps must be taken to prevent leakage from the bottom, but if the pond is spring-fed a small amount of leakage is a matter of no great import. The flow into and out of the pond must be such as to prevent stagnation and keep the water fresh and clear.

Sometimes inlets and promontories are made to vary the shoreline, and stones may be set in the middle of the pond. The embankment most often consists of stone groupings, although beaches of sand or gravel sloping into the water may also be used. From place to place, aquatic or marsh plants may be set along the shore. Here again, the designs are inspired by actual settings in nature.

The same can be said of artificial garden streams, which are most often modeled on rivulets flowing through forests and groves. Because of the influence it exerts on the whole garden, the width of the stream should be less than 2

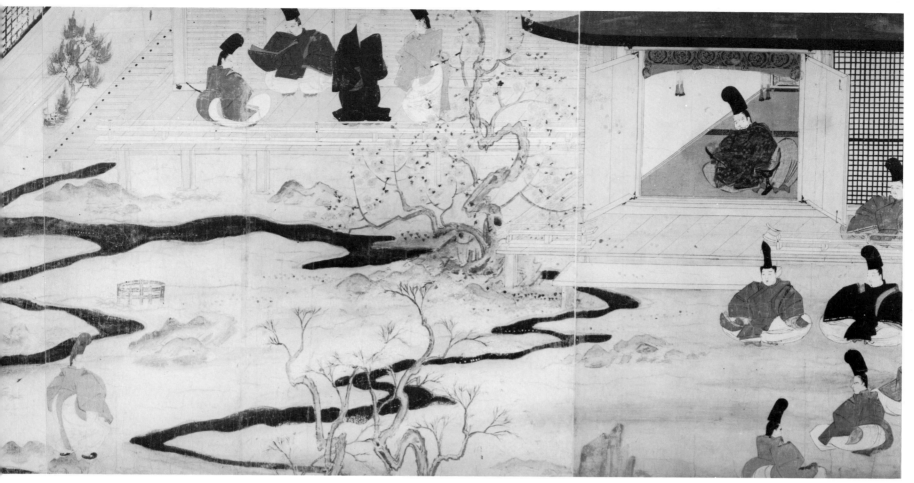

Scene of Heian courtiers and garden with plum and stream. (From a Kamakura-period scroll.)

meters; it should also be shallow, for the delightful and cooling effect of its murmuring as it ripples over the stones in its bed. Banks may be formed of stone, posts set at irregular heights, poles at uniform height, gravel, exposed earth, regular arrangements of roundish or flat stones, and so on. Some of these styles have already become things of the past; others are still, if rarely, used.

Unfortunately, it is difficult in Japan today to ensure supplies of pure, fresh water for gardens. Drilling wells for industrial and domestic use has so lowered the water table that additional wells for garden purposes are forbidden. Where rivers are polluted, it is generally necessary to rely on public waterworks and to use motor-driven pumps for fountains and waterfalls. In the modern world, the traditional Japanese garden is forced to make a determined fight for its very survival.

FENCES AND HEDGES

Let us imagine that I call on a person at home and speak with him without opening his door or actually seeing him. Did I meet that person? The old-fashioned, purely Japanese view would be that I did, because I spoke with him, even though I did not actually see his face. Prince Genji, the handsome eponymous hero of the celebrated Heian-period romance, wished to meet the Lady Hitachi; she was overjoyed at the idea, but hesitated because she lacked confidence in her own beauty. Her lady-in-waiting suggested an encounter in which the two would be on opposite sides of closed paper-covered partitions (*fusuma*). No Japanese of the time would have doubted that a true meeting had taken place.

Traditionally, the Japanese have had a dislike for complete partitioning in their residential architecture. The devices used to delineate space and to close one area off from another—sliding wooden doors, *fusuma*, or the still lighter paper-filled lattice panels called shoji—do not obstruct the passage of sound. Except when something like the danger of fire demands solid walls, the preference is for

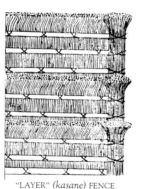

"LAYER" (*kasane*) FENCE

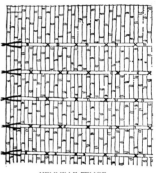

KENNIN-JI FENCE

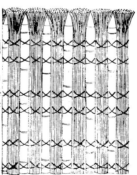

"RANK" (*tachiai*) FENCE

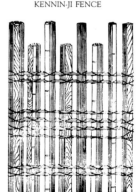

"CANNON" (*teppō*) SCREEN FENCE

"WHISK AND LATTICE" (*chasen-hishi*) SCREEN FENCE

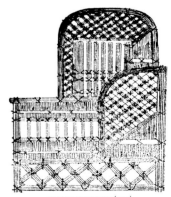

"EIGHT-STAGE" (*yae*) SCREEN FENCE

Garden Fences

"The Tale of Genji": visiting a lady. (From a late Heian-period scroll.)

spaces to be screened from sight but otherwise open to each other.

The Japanese garden fence is designed to satisfy this same preference. It is a partition, marking off the garden it belongs to from the adjacent plot, but in its simplest form—woven bamboo—it is more holes than structure, obstructs no sight or sound, and is usually low enough for an adult to leap over.

Sometimes high hedges are used in Japanese gardens. When the plants of which they are composed are thick with foliage, hedges block the lines of sight. High plank fences, too, effectively block the view, but even in such cases an attempt is made to establish a relation between the zones on either side. One way of doing this is to plant a tall, shapely pine by the fence. Passersby seeing the tree immediately imagine to themselves the lovely garden beyond, and perhaps even the life of the family owning it.

In short, like the partitions in traditional architecture, a Japanese garden fence and hedge is never a wall. It either allows sight and sound to pass through, or it stimulates the viewer in some way to envision what lies on its other side, thus generating a new kind of beauty.

In the Heian period, for example, the aristocrats were fond of viewing plum trees—at the time, exotic importations from China—through blinds made of extremely fine bamboo strips (*sudare*) and hung in the openings on all four sides of their buildings. The view of the trees was partially obstructed, and one was therefore free to flesh out the view with one's own imagination and create plum trees of a beauty vastly superior to reality.

Because hedges and fences are not really proof against possible intrusion and violation, they are practically never required to be either strong or durable. Consequently, they are most often made of relatively frail branches, bamboo, and grasses. Symbolic signs limit human motion in the Japanese garden more strongly than do some fences. The so-called boundary stone (*sekimori-ishi*) is a stone about 10 or 15 centimeters in diameter, bound in a cross with black

hemp rope and placed on a stepping stone in a tea-ceremony garden to indicate that the visitor must proceed no further in that direction. It can, of course, be ignored by visitors ignorant of its meaning, but the initiated always obey the injunction.

"BORROWED SCENERY"

In ancient Japan, there were beautiful views to be enjoyed in many places. Japanese garden designers, however, originally made no attempt to incorporate those views into their plans. The aristocrats of the Asuka and Nara periods (552–794) enjoyed the scenic beauty around them, but they prized much more highly certain famous landscapes at considerable distances from the Nara plain: Tamatsu Island in Kii (now Wakayama Prefecture), the Sumiyoshi Beach, the Seto Inland Sea, Mount Tateyama in Etchū (Toyama Prefecture), Mount Fuji in Suruga (Shizuoka Prefecture), Matsushima Bay in Mutsu (Miyagi Prefecture), and others.

Probably in about the tenth century, by which time the capital had been moved to what is now Kyoto, designers began to take note of particularly beautiful prospects in planning their residential gardens. An anecdote in a work called the *Ima kagami* (1170) about the retired emperor Goshirakawa and Tachibana no Toshitsuna, who wrote the *Sakutei-ki*, reveals how important the exterior view was to the gardens of the time. Goshirakawa had acquired the Toba Detached Palace, whose restoration we have already mentioned. Confident that his palace would head the list, Goshirakawa asked Toshitsuna to name the most outstanding gardens he knew. Toshitsuna put the Toba Detached Palace in third place, however, citing the palace's lack of good surrounding scenery.

Mountains, rivers, fields, the sea, thatched farmhouses, and peasants working in the paddy fields—all of which were gradually disappearing from the lives of city dwellers as urbanization progressed—were considered to make one's surroundings "scenic." The attitude of the aristocracy toward the peasants is interesting for the light it sheds on

"Borrowed scenery" at the Hōjō garden of Daitoku-ji, Kyoto.
(From an Edo-period guidebook.)

Jōju-in garden. Kiyomizu-dera, Kyoto.

the later seizure of power by the warrior class. The court nobles regarded farmhouses and hard-working, tax-paying peasants as mere decoration; they incorporated views of them into their garden but ignored them in their consideration of justice. The aristocracy, in other words, was aesthetically attuned but politically negligent, and this is part of the complex of reasons that later contributed to their fall from power.

By the thirteenth century, the warrior class was in firm control; the center of political administration had been moved to Kamakura, on the eastern seaboard, not far from modern Tokyo. The emperor retained his symbolic position, however, and the court was still the font from which flowed the honors and titles the powerful warrior class desired. The urbanization of Kyoto had reached a level at which the court nobles were compelled to construct villas in the suburbs if they wanted scenic surroundings for their garden designs. In the autumn of 1279, for example, records indicate that the retired emperors Gofukakusa and Kameyama visited a villa called the Fushimi Palace on the outskirts of the city. Although completely redone by this time, the Fushimi garden had originally been designed by Tachibana no Toshitsuna and was celebrated for its beauty. Chrysanthemums were in flower, and the maples were in full autumn foliage. The pair of emperors enjoyed the beauty of the sparkling white thread of the Uji River snaking its way through the distant plains from the mountains beyond. On the night of December 15 of the following year, a Buddhist memorial service was held at the Fushimi Palace; the participants were able to experience the harmony of the garden and its surroundings as the moon fell reflecting on the waters of a pond fringed with dried pampas grass. The sound of falling water could be heard from among the mountain boulders, and the pines made black silhouettes against the eaves of the building. In general, throughout the Kamakura period (1185–1333), natural scenery was deliberately included in designs as a garden element requiring no human management.

We have already noted that when the rivalry between the Northern and Southern imperial courts ended, the shogun Ashikaga Takauji built the temple Tenryū-ji and had Musō Soseki create a garden there for the repose of the spirit of his enemy, the emperor Godaigo of the Southern court. Traces of that garden still exist: it was a composition of pond, stone groups, and low hills that "borrowed" a variety of elements from the landscape: the Oi River, flowing beside the compound; the wooden Togetsu Bridge spanning the river; the mountain called Arashiyama in the distance. To recall the cherry trees of Mount Yoshino, where the Southern court had taken refuge, and the maples of Tatsuta, which was under the control of the Southern faction, Musō Soseki had Arashiyama planted with both trees. Yoshino and Tatsuta have been famous in Japanese poetry from ancient times, and it is said that Musō Soseki himself wrote poetry as he looked out on snow-capped Arashiyama from the garden of the Tenryū-ji, where he lived at the time.

In the late sixteenth and seventeenth century, the warring that had torn the nation apart for a long time ceased; the establishment of the Tokugawa shogunate in Edo brought a period of peace that was to last three centuries. To strengthen its hold over them, the Tokugawa government ordered the feudal lords all to build sumptuous residences in Edo and live there for specified periods, dividing their time between the capital and their own fiefs. Naturally all of these residences had gardens; and it was for their design and construction that the use of the surrounding landscape developed into a definite technique, which has come to be called *shakkei*, or "borrowed scenery." The borrowings included Mount Fuji, Edo Bay to the south of the city, and the Sumida River on the east. The gardeners doing this work did not use the Sino-Japanese term *shakkei* to describe the technique but preferred the word *ikedori*, which literally means "to take alive," as in the capture of animals. The following are four of the devices they used.

"Borrowed scenery" at Furumine Shrine, Ibaragi.

(1) Stone lanterns. At the Jōju-in abbot's residence of the temple Kiyomizu-dera, in Kyoto, the waters of a stream feed the small pond in a front garden. In the distance can be seen the Yuya valley and a ridge of mountains so undistinguished that it can do no more by itself than serve as a backdrop. In about the beginning of the seventeenth century, however—or so it is thought—a priest from the temple set a stone lantern in the middle of the ridge; by seeming to form a pair with a small stone lantern beside the pond, it creates the illusion that the hills are part of the garden composition.

(2) Tree trunks. In the early part of the seventeenth century, the temple Entsū-ji, in the northern suburbs of Kyoto, was part of a villa belonging to the emperor Gomizuno-o. The garden is a classic example of borrowed scenery, in this case consisting of three scenes in combination. The distant view is of Mount Hiei. The near view is of the small garden composed of forty stones, moss, and a few plants in front of the Entsū-ji main hall. The middle view is defined by a few cedar and cryptomeria cypress trees planted outside the hedge on the far side of the garden. The trees are clearly the intermediate element binding the near garden with the borrowed view of the mountain.

(3) Posts and eaves. At the Jikō-in, a small temple on a hill at Yamato Koizumi, the main hall is built in a style reminiscent of farmhouse architecture and does not look Buddhist at all. As one climbs the inclining approach, nothing can be seen but trees. Then, at the top of the hill, one goes through the two-story gate and into the main building to be suddenly confronted with a sweeping view of the fields, villages, and groves of the Yamato plain, a distant range of mountains, and the sky, through two full-width openings. Closer at hand is the garden in front of the main hall—spread with white gravel, set with stepping stones, and planted with azaleas that bloom in May. The lines of the posts and verandas on the two open sides frame the view and make it part of the garden.

(4) The sky. In traditional Oriental painting, blank spaces are of great importance in the way they fuse with the areas of pictorial representation to form a complete whole. The Kami-no-chaya, the uppermost section of the three-level garden of the Shugakuin Detached Palace in the northeastern suburbs of Kyoto, is a classic example of the use of blank space in garden design. In this case, the sky—which may, of course, be gray and overcast on gloomy days or highlighted with clouds—is the blank space in the composition. Below it are plains and ranges of mountains, and still closer at hand is the stroll garden of the villa itself. The emptiness of the sky is the link between the distant mountains, the pond, and the other elements of the garden.

Gardens are found throughout Japan, although the center
of garden art is unquestionably the old capital city of
Kyoto. The book ends with a selection of the author's
personal favorites—gardens from old to new,
reflecting the tastes of warriors, priests,
aristocrats, connoisseurs of tea, and country
landowners—with comments and practical information
for viewing and appreciation.

50 GARDENS: A SELECTION

Daisen-in. Shown here is one of the most famous stones in Japan. Shaped like a junk, it rides as it has since the 1500s in a dry-landscape river, a symbol of the passage of human life. The east garden of Daisen-in is one of the finest examples of how Chinese painting styles were used to construct miniature universes that served as objects of allegory and Zen contemplation. (Kyoto)

Katsura Detached Palace. Katsura is a visual delight, from its details of rockwork, stone lanterns, and refined decor to the more sublime blendings of structure and landscape. A long path of stepping stones—an expanded tea-garden roji—takes the visitor around the pond, while rustic pavilions along the way offer pleasing vistas and superb architectural variety. This was an aristocrat's country retreat, and the keynote here is unhurried elegance. (Kyoto)

Ryōan-ji. Considerably more abstract than the Daisen-in's miniature landscape, built at about the same time, the spare design of Ryōan-ji appeals greatly to modern tastes. It was, in fact, paid little attention until about the 1930s. Now, if anything, it suffers from hordes of tourists and overexplanation. The "meaning" of the garden has never been clear to anyone, and it should be enough to admire its superb rhythms and balance. (Kyoto)

Shugakuin Detached Palace. Upper Villa. The spectacular view to the west from the pavilion Rin'un-tei joins the manmade Pond of the Bathing Dragon with the distant hills by means of an overreaching sky. Such a grand scale is quite unusual in the Japanese gardening tradition, but it somehow fits the flamboyant personality of the owner of this estate, the retired emperor Gomizuno-o (1596-1680), who came here often for boating and other rural amusements. (Kyoto)

Shōden-ji. Large trimmed azaleas in boulderlike clumps of three, five, and seven are arranged in a rectangular gravel bed. This garden is particularly valued for its soothing composition and the way it harmonizes with the surrounding vegetation and the distant view of Mount Hiei. This highlights the effectiveness of the wall in the Japanese garden as a background support that mediates between inside and outside. (Kyoto)

Rokuon-ji (Kinkaku-ji). Shogun Ashikaga Yoshimitsu (1358-1408) built a villa for himself west of the capital on land that had once served as a pond-and-temple garden for the powerful Saionji family. Yoshimitsu retained the pond, and on its edge he built the Golden Pavilion, which he used for entertaining, contemplation, and, of course, viewing the surrounding landscape. The pond's main island is planted with pines and rimmed with stone compositions to be enjoyed while boating. (Kyoto)

Konchi-in. This garden dates from 1627 and is the work of artist-designer Kobori Enshū. Enshū here substituted plantings on a hillside for the garden wall. The flat stone is designed for standing on to admire the Tōshōgū, a shrine dedicated to the first Tokugawa shogun, Ieyasu. But it is an important design element as well, tying the left and right halves of the garden together. (Kyoto)

Tenryū-ji. This famous stone grouping is frequently said to look good no matter what direction it is viewed from. It uses the pond as both reflective surface and as horizontal plane to enhance the sculpture. On a literal level it represents the mystic island of Hōrai, but it also echoes and draws the eyes to the hills that surround the garden. Multifunctionalism creates depth of meaning and unity of design. (Kyoto)

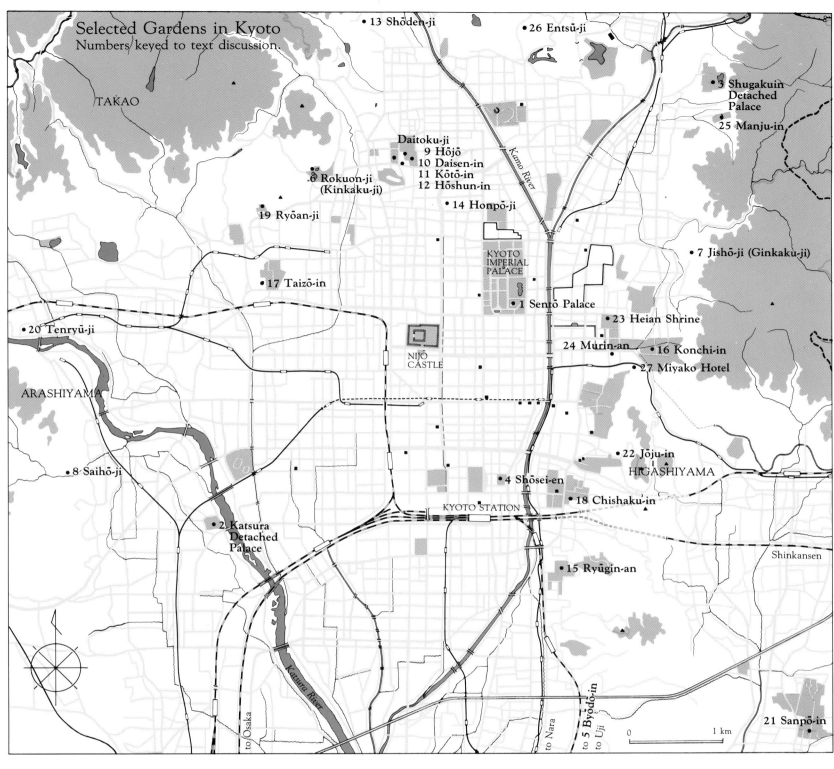

Selected Gardens in Kyoto
Numbers keyed to text discussion.

• 13 Shōden-ji

• 26 Entsū-ji

TAKAO

• 3 Shugakuin Detached Palace

• 25 Manju-in

Daitoku-ji
  9 Hōjō
  10 Daisen-in
  11 Kōtō-in
  12 Hōshun-in

Kamo River

• 6 Rokuon-ji (Kinkaku-ji)

• 19 Ryōan-ji

• 14 Honpō-ji

KYOTO IMPERIAL PALACE

• 7 Jishō-ji (Ginkaku-ji)

• 17 Taizō-in

• 1 Sentō Palace

• 20 Tenryū-ji

• 23 Heian Shrine

24 Murin-an • • 16 Konchi-in

NIJŌ CASTLE

• 27 Miyako Hotel

ARASHIYAMA

• 8 Saihō-ji

• 22 Jōju-in

HIGASHIYAMA

• 4 Shōsei-en

• 18 Chishaku-in

KYOTO STATION

• 2 Katsura Detached Palace

• 15 Ryūgin-an

Shinkansen

Katsura River

to Osaka

to Nara

to 5 Byōdō-in

to Uji

• 21 Sanpō-in

0   1 km

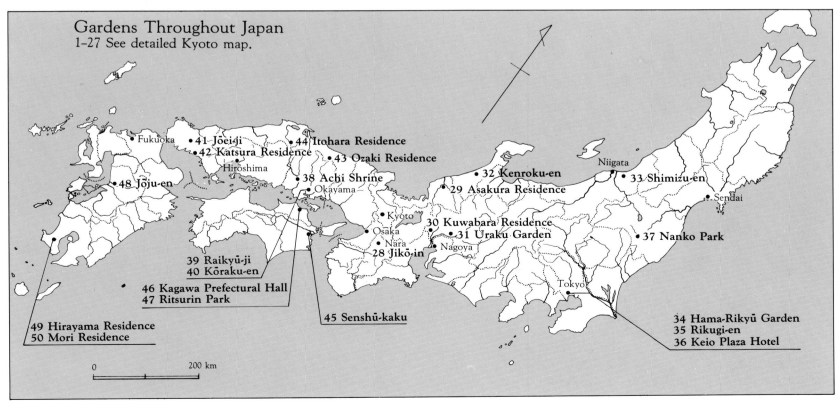

Gardens Throughout Japan
1–27 See detailed Kyoto map.

• Fukuoka

• 41 Jōei-ji

• 44 Itohara Residence

• 42 Katsura Residence

• 43 Ozaki Residence

Hiroshima

• 48 Jōju-en

• 38 Achi Shrine

• 32 Kenroku-en

Niigata

• 33 Shimizu-en

Okayama

• 29 Asakura Residence

Sendai

• Kyoto

• 30 Kuwabara Residence

• Osaka

• 31 Uraku Garden

• 37 Nanko Park

• Nara

• Nagoya

• 28 Jikō-in

39 Raikyū-ji
40 Kōraku-en

46 Kagawa Prefectural Hall
47 Ritsurin Park

Tokyo

45 Senshū-kaku

34 Hama-Rikyū Garden
35 Rikugi-en
36 Keio Plaza Hotel

49 Hirayama Residence
50 Mori Residence

0   200 km

The material here is intended for readers who plan to visit Japan and want to spend some of their time there viewing gardens. A few general observations: Every effort has been made to provide accurate, up-to-date information in these listings. Admission fees change frequently, however, and access to gardens may be restricted owing to holidays, special functions, or construction work. While photography is generally permitted, many gardens will forbid your using tripods and taking pictures indoors. At gardens maintained by the Imperial Household Agency, you will be escorted in groups that leave at appointed times; latecomers are not admitted. At most other gardens, you can spend as much or as little time as you please. Temples will normally not permit you to enter the garden area, while large stroll gardens are more like public parks. Picnicking and smoking are, of course, restricted. For your reference, the names and addresses of the gardens are given here in Japanese as well as English. Gardens listed as being not open to the general public can sometimes be seen by special permission of the owners; try to make your request in writing well in advance of your travel. More

information about the gardens is available from the garden offices; since few places have English-speaking staff, you should try to find someone to speak on your behalf in Japanese.

Listings include data, brief descriptions, and general comments. Page references here are to color captions and black-and-white illustrations in this book. Dates of construction generally refer to the period when major work was first carried out on the garden. Not all scholars would choose the same date. Furthermore, gardens change over time, and what is on view today is often considerably different from what was originally planned. In particular, the constant presence of hordes of tourists has caused some gardens to take steps to protect their holdings, by laying in guardrails and asphalt paths, or to cater to commercial concerns, by installing vending machines and intrusive loudspeakers. One final note: this is a personal selection and is not intended as a guide to all the major gardens in Japan. Particularly in Kyoto, you will find many more places worth visiting near the ones mentioned here. Consult other maps and guidebooks for further information.

1. SENTŌ PALACE
仙洞御所

Kyōto Gyoen-nai, Kamigyō-ku, Kyoto 602
〒602 京都市上京区京都御苑内

☎ 075-211-1211

stroll garden

early Edo period

HOURS: Tours at prescribed times Monday–Saturday. Closed Saturday afternoon, Sunday, national holidays, and before and after New Year (December 25–January 5). Apply to Imperial Household Agency at Kyoto Imperial Palace in advance of visit (telephone number as listed above).

ADMISSION FEE: None.
PHOTOGRAPHY: Permitted.
NOTE: A path leads around a northern and southern pond, presenting the viewer with constantly shifting panoramas as it winds along a gently sloped area of lawn, by a waterfall, over a bridge, under a wisteria trellis. The scalloped cobblestone beach on the southern pond is much admired. See pages 40, 216.

In 1629, angered by the policies of the Tokugawa shogunal government, the emperor Gomizuno-o abdicated. This residence and its gardens, created in 1633 under the guidance of Kobori Enshū, are thought to have been part of a construction program intended to appease the retired emperor. Over the years, the garden has changed so much that practically nothing remains of Kobori Enshū's original design. Nonetheless, the general harmony of the composition has persisted in a way characteristic of Japanese gardens: they live because they change.

2. KATSURA DETACHED PALACE
桂離宮

Katsura Misono, Nishigyō-ku, Kyoto 615
〒615 京都市西京区桂御園
☎ 075-381-2029

stroll garden

early Edo period

HOURS: Tours at prescribed times Monday–Saturday. Closed Saturday afternoon, Sunday, national holidays, and before and after New Year (December 25–January 5). Apply to Imperial Household Agency at Kyoto Imperial Palace in advance of visit (tel: 075-211-1211).
ADMISSION FEE: None.
PHOTOGRAPHY: Permitted.

NOTE: A complete stroll garden combining the forms and methods of a pond garden, stone-and-gravel garden, and tea-garden roji. The main structures (Old Shoin, Middle Shoin, New Palace) are integrated with smaller pavilions ranged around a central pond. Katsura is particularly famous for its variety of stone pavements. All the buildings are original, and the Shoin area has just been restored. See pages 4, 73, 89, 184, 192.

First called a "detached palace" of the imperial household only a century ago, Katsura was originally a country retreat of the princes of the Hachijō line, who were later named the Katsura princes. Its grounds include the oldest extant versions of the stroll garden and still convey a good sense of the intentions of their creators, the first Hachijō prince, Toshihito, and his son, Toshitada. Lovely in itself, the garden was planned to evoke such works of classical Japanese literature as *The Tale of Genji* and therefore, as is typical of aristocratic gardens, can be understood fully only by people with the requisite education.

3. SHUGAKUIN DETACHED PALACE
修学院離宮

Shugakuin, Sakyō-ku, Kyoto 606
〒606 京都市左京区修学院
☎ 075-781-5203

stroll garden
early Edo period

HOURS: Tours at prescribed times Monday–Saturday. Closed Saturday afternoon, Sunday, national holidays, and before and after New Year (December 25–January 5). Apply to Imperial Household Agency at Kyoto Imperial Palace in advance of visit (tel: 075-211-1211).
ADMISSION FEE: None.
PHOTOGRAPHY: Permitted.

BEST TIME TO VISIT: Autumn, for the colorful leaves.
NOTE: An element of surprise is built into the design of the garden. The path leading to the pavilion Rin'un-tei on the Upper Villa rises through a corridor cut into a tall hedge. Suddenly the visitor emerges into the open—before him is the spectacular view across to the hills in the north and west. See pages 3, 88, 192.

Vast by Japanese standards, Shugakuin consists of three gardens arranged among paddy fields on a gentle slope. In days gone by, court nobles in search of rural scenes enjoyed the cherries of spring, the greenery of summer, the brilliant foliage of autumn, and the snowscapes of winter as they strolled from garden to garden on raised paths, and picked wild flowers and herbs in season. All of the garden buildings are small and subtly refined.

4. SHŌSEI-EN AT HIGASHI-HONGAN-JI 東本願寺渉成園

Ainomachi, Higashi Tamamizu-chō, Shimogyō-ku, Kyoto 606
〒606 京都市下京区東玉水町間之町
☎ 075-371-9181

pond-and-island garden
originally Heian period

HOURS: 9:00–4:00.
ADMISSION FEE: None.
PHOTOGRAPHY: Permitted.
BEST TIME TO VISIT: Spring, for the cherry blossoms.

NOTE: A level site is filled with a large pond and islands. There are various tea pavilions, covered bridges, and towers. Trees include cherry, plum, wisteria, maple.

Sometime in the ninth century, Minister of the Left Minamoto no Tōru is said to have built a villa for himself on the site of this garden, and re-created in the bed of the Kamo River a scene of the primitive salt fields at Shiogama near Matsushima Bay in northeastern Japan. In the early part of the seventeenth century a samurai named Ishikawa Jōzan, known for his cultural attainments, had the gardens created approximately as they are today. The pond is dotted with islands, some representing the tortoise and crane, traditionally auspicious animals in Japan, and others symbolizing the Islands of the Blessed, an imported Chinese tradition.

5. BYŌDŌ-IN
平等院

Ujirenge-chō, Uji-shi, Kyoto 611
〒611 京都府宇治市宇治蓮華町
☎ 0774-22-3920

paradise garden
Heian period

HOURS: 9:00–4:00.
ADMISSION FEE: ¥300.
PHOTOGRAPHY: Permitted. No indoor flash, no tripods.

NOTE: The temple is on a site above the Uji River and affords a good view of Mount Asahi. An Amida hall flanked by corridors on a central island makes a fine evocation of the Buddha's Western Paradise. See pages 28, 79.

Today a Buddhist temple, this was in the eleventh century a villa of the regent Fujiwara no Yorimichi. The villa was ostensibly built as an act of faith, centered—as was usual at the time—on a Buddhist hall, and meant to be an earthly representation of the Western Paradise of the Buddha Amida. Later, everything was destroyed in war except the Amida hall and the pond, which symbolizes the Pond of the Seven Precious Substances. At night, and with a good imagination, the visitor can picture the villa in its days of glory.

6. ROKUON-JI (KINKAKU-JI)
鹿苑寺（金閣寺）

1 Kinkaku-ji-chō, Kita-ku, Kyoto 603
〒603 京都市北区金閣寺町 1

☎ 075-461-0013

pond-and-island garden
Kamakura period

HOURS: 9:00–5:30 (April 1–September 30).
9:00–5:00 (October 1–March 31).
ADMISSION FEE: ¥500.
PHOTOGRAPHY: Permitted.
BEST TIME TO VISIT: Autumn, and after a
snowfall in winter.

NOTE: The three-tiered Golden Pavilion is the
focus of the garden. It exerts a unifying force
on the expansive view of the broad Mirror Lake
that spreads out beneath it, partly due to the
skillful placement of crags and islands. A path
behind leads through a leafy forest. See pages
106, 192.

In the thirteenth century, this property was the villa of a court noble named Saionji Kin-
tsune. In the fourteenth century, it was purchased by the shogun Ashikaga Yoshimitsu
and extensively redone. At Yoshimitsu's death his villa became the temple today known
as the Rokuon-ji. The only thing remaining of the villa now is the lake. The famous Golden
Pavilion—or Kinkaku, from which the popular name of the temple derives—was destroyed
by fire in 1950 and reconstructed in 1955.

7. JISHŌ-JI (GINKAKU-JI)
慈照寺（銀閣寺）

Ginkaku-ji-chō, Sakyō-ku, Kyoto 606
〒606 京都市左京区銀閣寺町

☎ 075-771-5725

paradise garden
Muromachi period

HOURS: 8:30–5:00 (March 15–November 30).
9:00–4:30 (December 1–March 14).
ADMISSION FEE: ¥150.
PHOTOGRAPHY: Permitted.
BEST TIME TO VISIT: Autumn.

NOTE: Raked and molded gravel mounds represent the sea and a mountain. A path climbs the
hill behind to a spring. The approachway is
noteworthy for its fence combining stone, bamboo, and hedge. The temple says that a building
behind the main hall contains Japan's first tea
room. See pages 102, 171, 182.

Like the Rokuon-ji, or Kinkaku-ji, the Jishō-ji is a temple that was formerly the villa of
a shogun. As a companion piece to the Golden Pavilion at Rokuon-ji, here there is a Silver
Pavilion (Ginkaku), although it is silver in name only as the owner, Ashikaga Yoshimasa,
died before the silver leaf could be applied. The most important objects to view here are
the broad gravel "sea" with rippling waves and the large truncated cone resembling Mount
Fuji just as you enter the main grounds. These were apparently installed by the samurai
Miyagi Toyomori about 130 years after the temple's establishment.

8. SAIHŌ-JI (KOKE-DERA)
西芳寺（苔寺）

Jingatani-chō, Matsuo, Ukyō-ku, Kyoto 615
〒615 京都市右京区松尾神ケ谷町

☎ 075-391-3631

paradise garden and dry-landscape garden
Kamakura period

HOURS: Tours conducted at times specified by
the temple. Apply by postcard only, at least
three days in advance.
ADMISSION FEE: ¥3,000.
PHOTOGRAPHY: Permitted. No tripods.
BEST TIME TO VISIT: Spring, rainy season in June,
autumn.

NOTE: An almost primordial lower garden consisting of a large pond with islands and banks
covered in lush moss. A path leads up a hill to
a spectacular dry-landscape cascade. Before
viewing the garden you are asked to attend a
sutra-reading at the main hall for about half an
hour. See pages 40, 92, 101–10.

Apparently Saihō-ji was once so splendid that it provided the model for the Temple of
the Silver Pavilion (Ginkaku-ji). The garden was repeatedly damaged by fire and flood
from the fourteenth century on; by the eighteenth century, it was a wreck inhabited by
only one monk. The trees grew rank, and mosses covered the ground. Ultimately, the
mosses were allowed to grow unhampered, giving the temple the name by which it is most
famous now: the Koke-dera, or Moss Temple.

9. PRINCIPAL QUARTERS OF THE DAITOKU-JI HŌJŌ 大徳寺本坊

Daitoku-ji-chō, Murasakino, Kita-ku, Kyoto 603
〒603 京都市北区紫野大徳寺町
☎ 075–491–0019

dry-landscape garden
early Edo period

Not open to the general public.

NOTE: Two cone-shaped "mountains" rise out of a gravel "sea." They are thought to derive from piles of gravel kept on hand to replenish the garden on special occasions. See page 189.

The Daitoku-ji is a collection of subtemples used for study and meditation by monks of the Rinzai sect of Zen Buddhism. The Hōjō is its principal building. The typical Zen-style stone-and-gravel garden here was created by Gyokushitsu Sōhaku when he returned from five years of exile in the northeastern part of Honshu—a sentence imposed in 1629 for a breach of shogunate law. The white gravel covering most of the plot is raked into patterns. There are two large stones near the veranda of the abbot's quarters and a number of other stones opposite in the southeast corner. Two other stones standing in camellias pruned to suggest a flow of water provide a pleasing accent to the spacious, simple design.

10. DAISEN-IN AT DAITOKU-JI 大仙院

Daitoku-ji-chō, Murasakino, Kita-ku, Kyoto 603
〒603 京都市北区紫野大徳寺町
☎ 075–491–8346

dry-landscape garden
Muromachi period

HOURS: 9:00–5:00 (until 4:30 in winter).
ADMISSION FEE: ¥300.
PHOTOGRAPHY: Permitted. No tripods.

NOTE: The wall that divides the east garden in two was installed in recent times after checking sources on the site's original appearance. Note the famous boat-shaped rock. See pages 40, 175.

There are two gardens at the subtemple Daisen-in. One of them is purely symbolic and abstract, consisting only of white gravel raked into patterns and accented by two white-gravel mounds. This garden is in front of the main hall. The other, a small garden on the east of the main hall, consists of gravel, stones, and a few plants. The design suggests a stream flowing from remote mountains toward the sea, and expresses the typical Zen belief that even a small plot can be a universe in microcosm.

11. KŌTŌ-IN AT DAITOKU-JI 高桐院

Daitoku-ji-chō, Murasakino, Kita-ku, Kyoto 603
〒603 京都市北区紫野大徳寺町
☎ 075–492–0068

dry-landscape garden
late Edo period

HOURS: 9:00–4:30.
ADMISSION FEE: ¥300.
PHOTOGRAPHY: Permitted.
BEST TIME TO VISIT: Early summer, autumn.

NOTE: The right-angled approachway of natural stone is interesting for the leisurely way it prepares the visitor for entry into the grounds proper. At the very rear of the site is a teahouse and various tea gardens dotted with numerous lanterns and basins. Unlike at most temples, you can wander to examine the settings close up. The temple is very popular in November when the maple leaves are at their best. See page 112.

Because it must serve as a setting for various ceremonies, the area in front of the main hall of a Buddhist temple is usually covered with gravel and planted with no more than a very few trees. The garden of the temple Kōtō-in, however, boasts a grove of maples that are green from spring through summer and brilliant red in the fall. In winter, the blue sky and scudding white clouds can be seen through the bare branches. I recall once being tired from walking and stopping to admire the dim, almost gloomy, shadows cast by the maples in summer.

12. HŌSHUN-IN AT DAITOKU-JI
芳春院

Daitoku-ji-chō, Murasakino, Kita-ku, Kyoto 603 ☎ 075-492-6010
〒603 京都市北区紫野大徳寺町

dry-landscape garden and pond garden
early Edo period

HOURS: 8:30–4:00. Closed the 1st and 15th of every month.
ADMISSION FEE: ¥200.
PHOTOGRAPHY: Permitted.
BEST TIME TO VISIT: Late summer to early autumn.

NOTE: The dry-landscape is of a stream emerging from a mountain ravine into a lake which empties into the vast sea. Behind the main hall and overlooking a real pond is a two-story structure, the Donkokaku, built in 1617. See page 173.

My own feeling is that this garden was made to be seen exclusively in early autumn, when the Chinese bell flowers in front of the temple hall are in bloom. Gardens graced with flowers all the year round are pleasant, but so are gardens like this, where the blossoms appear in one season only. Perhaps the Chinese bell flowers were selected to symbolize blooms of all kinds.

13. SHŌDEN-JI
正伝寺

Chinjuan-chō, Nishigamo, Kita-ku, Kyoto 603 ☎ 075-491-3259
〒603 京都市北区西加茂鎮守庵町

dry-landscape garden
early Edo period

HOURS: 9:00–5:00.
ADMISSION FEE: ¥200.
PHOTOGRAPHY: Permitted.
BEST TIME TO VISIT: Spring, for the azaleas, and autumn.

NOTE: Pruned azaleas are arranged in clumps of 3, 5, and 7, a typical configuration usually applied to rockwork, as seen at the Shinju-an. On clear days, Mount Hiei is visible in the background. See page 192.

With its inconvenient location in the hills on the northern outskirts of the city, the Shōden-ji usually has few visitors, but during the student protests of the 1960s many frustrated young people reportedly came here for quiet thought and reflection. I also have been wrapped in contemplation of the simple white gravel and pruned azaleas of the garden, the blue sky beyond, and the long vista of days past.

14. HONPŌ-JI
本法寺

Teranouchi-agaru, Ogawa-dōri, Kamigyō-ku, Kyoto 602 ☎ 075-441-7997
〒602 京都市上京区小川通寺之内上ル

dry-landscape garden
early Edo period

HOURS: 9:00–5:00.
ADMISSION FEE: ¥100–200.
PHOTOGRAPHY: Permitted.

NOTE: The design comprises three comma-shaped clipped hedges in the space surrounded by the Hōjō, Kuri, and the Hōzō (the building where the temple's valuables are kept). In the southeast corner is a dry-landscape waterfall, below which is a famous stone bridge.

The garden was created in the early seventeenth century by Hon'ami Kōetsu, who was by profession an appraiser of swords and by avocation an outstanding calligrapher and tea master. Originally the small pond in the foreground next to the Hōjō was octagonal in shape, planted with lotuses, and faced with cut stones—which are rarely used in traditional Japanese gardens. Today, however, though still lined with cut stones, it is decagonal, planted with iris, and surprisingly modern in appearance.

15. RYŪGIN-AN AT TŌFUKU-JI
竜吟庵

15 Honmachi, Higashiyama-ku, Kyoto 605
〒605 京都市東山区本町 15

☎ 075-541-8972

dry-landscape garden
modern period

HOURS: 9:00–4:00. Open only in November.
ADMISSION FEE: ¥300.
PHOTOGRAPHY: Permitted.

NOTE: This is the work of Shigemori Mirei, a garden historian and one of the foremost exponents of modern Japanese garden design. Other Shigemori gardens are nearby at the Hōjō of the Tōfuku-ji.

Hidden behind the main hall of the Zen temple Tōfuku-ji, this subtemple is difficult to find and thus quiet and secluded. It must have had influential supporters at one time to make possible the four entirely different stone-and-gravel gardens surrounding the main hall, one on each side. Three of the four were reconstructed by Shigemori Mirei since the end of World War II, but each has a strong and distinct personality of its own.

16. KONCHI-IN AT NANZEN-JI
金地院

Fukuchi-chō, Nanzen-ji, Sakyō-ku, Kyoto 606
〒606 京都市左京区南禅寺福地町

☎ 075-771-3511

dry-landscape garden and pond garden
early Edo period

HOURS: 8:00–5:00.
ADMISSION FEE: ¥300.
PHOTOGRAPHY: Permitted.
BEST TIME TO VISIT: Early summer, autumn.

NOTE: A large "worship" stone with a scene of the mystic island of Hōrai in the background and, in front, a gravel area in a boat shape. A fine example of the early Edo style. See page 192.

Kobori Enshū, whose work this garden clearly is, was a cultivated man and a shogunal official. He was commissioned to do this design by the Zen priest Konchi'in Sūden, an advisor to the shogun's family. While making its own strong personal statement, the garden simultaneously expresses an attitude of respect for those of high estate: the use of elements with connotations of good fortune, such as the artificial hillocks representing the tortoise and the crane—both symbols of long life—and a flat stone from which to admire the Tō-shōgū Shrine, devoted to the Tokugawa family and especially its founder, Ieyasu. As is typical of Kobori Enshū, however, there is nothing servile about the design.

17. TAIZŌ-IN AT MYŌSHIN-JI
退蔵院

35 Myōshin-ji-chō, Hanazono, Ukyō-ku, Kyoto 616
〒616 京都市右京区花園妙心寺町 35

☎ 075-463-2855

dry-landscape garden
Muromachi period

HOURS: 9:00–5:00.
ADMISSION FEE: ¥300.
PHOTOGRAPHY: Permitted.
BEST TIME TO VISIT: Late summer.

NOTE: An easy-to-appreciate rendering of the natural world. Down the hill from the temple is a modern-day garden by Kyoto designer Nakane Kinsaku.

Kanō Motonobu (1476–1559), a prominent artist of the famous Kanō school, is said to have designed the realistic stone-and-gravel garden on the western side of the Hōjō in about 1520. The composition includes an expanse of white sand representing water, stones representing a waterfall and a pond, an island symbolizing a tortoise, a stone bridge, and background planting; it suggests the work of a landscape painter. The design and the tradition of calling this "Motonobu's Garden" reinforce the attribution.

18. CHISHAKU-IN
智積院

Shichijō, Higashiyama, Higashiyama-ku, Kyoto 605
〒605 京都市東山区東山七条 ☎ 075-541-5361

stone-and-pond garden
Momoyama period

HOURS: 9:00–4:30. Closed every Monday and December 28–January 6.
ADMISSION FEE: ¥300.
PHOTOGRAPHY: Permitted (garden only).
BEST TIME TO VISIT: May and June, for the azaleas.

NOTE: Very good use of spatial effects. Distances appear much greater as the eye scans the hillside or follows the water beyond the bridge and off into the distance. The construction is noteworthy for the way the pond here actually comes under the building. See page 217.

The wide garden here makes use of a slope that leads to a guest house. At the bottom of the incline, which is planted with flowering shrubbery—mainly azaleas—is a pond fed by a natural spring and spanned by a bridge of bluish stone. Once when I visited the garden, the azaleas flashed and reflected on the surfaces of stones and boulders wet by a quiet rain.

19. RYŌAN-JI
竜安寺

Goryōshitano-chō, Ryōan-ji, Ukyō-ku, Kyoto 616
〒616 京都市右京区竜安寺御陵下ノ町 ☎ 075-463-2216

dry-landscape garden
Muromachi (early Edo?) period

HOURS: 8:00–5:00.
ADMISSION FEE: ¥200.
PHOTOGRAPHY: Permitted.

NOTE: The Ryōan-ji is on everybody's itinerary and gets very crowded and noisy, especially when schoolchildren come to visit. Early morning is usually safe, although you may have to endure a loudspeaker relentlessly "explaining" what the garden is all about. See pages 81, 172, 192.

The moss by the boulders in this typical stone-and-gravel garden sprang up naturally. No one seems to know precisely what the fifteen stones set in the expanse of white gravel are supposed to represent; nor is a clear answer necessary. Perhaps the garden was meant as a kind of *kōan*, one of the enigmatic questions whereby Zen priests attempt to stimulate enlightenment in their trainees.

20. TENRYŪ-JI
天竜寺

Susukinobaba-chō, Tenryū-ji, Saga, Ukyō-ku, Kyoto 616
〒616 京都市右京区嵯峨天竜寺芒ノ馬場町 ☎ 075-881-1235

pond garden
Kamakura period

HOURS: 8:30–5:00.
ADMISSION FEE: ¥350.
PHOTOGRAPHY: Permitted.
BEST TIME TO VISIT: Early April, November.

NOTE: The garden is focused on a dry waterfall across the pond from the temple buildings. A stone on the lower level represents a carp that, according to legend, is trying to climb the falls and become a dragon. The stone bridge at the base of the falls is the oldest example extant. Bring a small pair of binoculars so that you can pick out the details. See pages 36, 40, 192, 216.

Inside the site are a pond and a stone group that doubles as a retaining embankment. Although traditional Japanese gardens often recall famous scenes in Japan, this one is modeled on Chinese ink paintings, possibly because trade with China was flourishing when it was designed. At the time the temple was established, the imperial court was split into the Northern court in Kyoto and the Southern court on Mount Yoshino. The famous warrior Ashikaga Takauji, who supported the Northern court, had the Tenryū-ji built as a memorial to his enemy, the emperor Godaigo of the Southern court.

21. SANPŌ-IN AT DAIGO-JI
三宝院

Daigo-ji, Higashiōji-chō, Daigo, Fushimi-ku, Kyoto 612
〒612 京都市伏見区醍醐東大路町醍醐
☎ 075-571-0002

stone-and-pond garden
Momoyama–early Edo period

HOURS: 9:00–4:00 (October–March). 9:00–5:00 (April–September).
ADMISSION FEE: ¥300.
PHOTOGRAPHY: Not permitted.
BEST TIME TO VISIT: Spring, for the azaleas, and November, for the autumn leaves.

NOTE: Seven hundred rocks are artfully arranged, including the famous Fujito stone with its long history. Earthen bridges are used here for the first time. The area around the Sanpō-in is very nice for hiking. See pages 5, 175.

In 1598 the military ruler of Japan, Toyotomi Hideyoshi, held a sumptuous cherry-viewing party on this site; in the twenty-odd years that followed, the garden achieved roughly its present form, with its pond, waterfall, islands, and plantings. Ordinarily a garden of this kind would be laid out to permit strolling, but the Sanpō-in garden is intended to be seen from seated positions in the rooms or verandas of the adjacent building. The combination of gravel and round patches of moss in one corner developed naturally, and was so admired that it was preserved that way.

22. JŌJU-IN AT KIYOMIZU-DERA
成就院

Kiyomizu, 1-chōme, Higashiyama-ku, Kyoto 605
〒605 京都市東山区清水一丁目
☎ 075-551-1234

pond-and-island garden
mid-Edo period

Not open to the general public.

NOTE: Two islands with striking rock formations call to mind the traditional tortoise and crane arrangements. The use of a "borrowed" landscape here, in addition to extending the garden spatially, adds a measure of richness to the scene as the view changes according to mist, rain, and snowfall. See page 189.

The Jōju-in garden has a pond brimming with sparkling water. Actually quite small, it "borrows" the Yuya valley and mountains in the distance: on the lower slope of the mountain is a stone lantern that, by seeming to be a part of the design, gives the illusion that the garden is much larger than it is.

23. HEIAN SHRINE
平安神宮

Nishitennō-chō, Okazaki, Sakyō-ku, Kyoto 606
〒606 京都市左京区岡崎西天王町
☎ 075-761-0221

stroll garden
Meiji period

HOURS: 8:30–4:30 (November–February). 8:30–5:00 (March 1–14, September–October). 8:30–5:30 (March 15–August).
ADMISSION FEE: ¥300.
PHOTOGRAPHY: Permitted.
BEST TIME TO VISIT: April, for the cherry blossoms in the East Garden.

NOTE: This is a rare example of an extensive pond garden on the grounds of a Shinto shrine. The forecourt is spread with white gravel, while the shrine building, a covered bridge, and a tower capped by a phoenix are used in the scenery of the stroll garden in back. The designer was Ogawa Jihei, who also worked on the Murin-an.

In 1894 celebrations were held to commemorate the 1,100th anniversary of Kyoto (once called Heian-kyō) as the imperial capital. The Heian Shrine, modeled on eighth-century designs, was built as part of those celebrations. To the east, west, and north of the shrine building are gardens designed fundamentally for strolling. One of the most notable features here is the stepping stones in the pond, actually the pillars of a sixteenth-century stone bridge that spanned the Kamo River until it was destroyed in an earthquake.

24. MURIN-AN
無鄰庵

Kusakawa-chō, Nanzen-ji, Sakyō-ku, Kyoto 606
〒606 京都市左京区南禅寺草川町

☎ 075-781-3909

stroll garden
Meiji period

HOURS: 9:00–12:00, 1:00–4:30. Closed Monday.
ADMISSION FEE: ¥200.
PHOTOGRAPHY: Permitted.
BEST TIME TO VISIT: Autumn.

NOTE: The wedge-shaped site is on a slight incline. A three-tiered waterfall brings water in to form a broad, shallow stream that twists its way down toward the buildings at the opposite end. There is a view of the eastern hills through the trees at the edge of the property. See page 90.

Apparently the idea of its owner, the statesman and military figure Yamagata Aritomo, the Murin-an garden marked a turning point in the history of Kyoto stroll gardens, especially as regards the non-traditional plant materials used. Ogawa Jihei, who was in charge of the actual construction, is said to have started work on the project in 1893, when he was only thirty-four years old. It was completed in 1896. Closely examined, the garden proves itself outstanding in its details, notably the handling of the stream, in addition to its overall conception. It became a model for gardens of this kind throughout the Kyoto region.

25. MANJU-IN
曼殊院

Takenouchi-chō, Ichijō, Sakyō-ku, Kyoto 606
〒606 京都市左京区一乗寺竹ノ内町

☎ 075-781-5010

dry-landscape garden
early Edo period

HOURS: 9:00–5:00.
ADMISSION FEE: ¥400.
PHOTOGRAPHY: Permitted.
BEST TIME TO VISIT: Spring, autumn.

NOTE: Try to view the garden from the interior of the building called the Small Shoin, where the sense of movement and spaciousness in the stone-and-gravel landscape is most striking. Islands include the traditional tortoise and crane groupings.

The second son of Toshihito, the Hachijō prince who built the Katsura villa, directed the making of this *kare sansui* garden, which dates from the middle of the seventeenth century. In an expanse of white gravel representing the sea are three islands with small stone towers, pine trees, tower-shaped stones, and stone groupings representing the Buddha and two attendant bodhisattvas. On spring evenings, azaleas in full bloom in the garden turn the white paper of the closed shoji panels a pale lavender.

26. ENTSŪ-JI
円通寺

Hataeda-chō, Iwakura, Sakyō-ku, Kyoto 606
〒606 京都市左京区岩倉幡枝町

☎ 075-781-1875

dry-landscape garden
early Edo period

HOURS: 10:00–4:00.
ADMISSION FEE: ¥300.
PHOTOGRAPHY: Not permitted.
BEST TIME TO VISIT: Clear days.

NOTE: You enter the building from the west and proceed along a narrow corridor until you have to turn left. At this point the garden comes into view for the first time. The effect is startling. See page 5.

This is the most typical extant example of a garden that figuratively "borrows" the distant scenery to form part of its own composition. Though they seem to have been set in place by design, the large stones in the area enclosed by a low hedge are actually the exposed tops of natural boulders. Distant Mount Hiei is visible through the trees planted outside the hedge: These trees are the medium the garden designer has used to capture the mountain and incorporate it in his composition.

27. MIYAKO HOTEL KASUI-EN ANNEX
都ホテル　佳水園

Keage, Sanjō, Higashiyama-ku, Kyoto 605
〒605　京都市東山区三条蹴上
☎ 075-771-7111

dry-landscape garden
modern period

HOURS: Open to hotel guests only.
ADMISSION FEE: None.
PHOTOGRAPHY: Permitted.

NOTE: The design shows mossy gourd-shaped islands in a gravel sea, closely resembling a garden on the upper level of Sanpō-in.

This modern stone-and-gravel garden was designed by the well-known architect Murano Tōgo, who did the hotel buildings as well. Materials are limited to white gravel and green moss, the most ordinary and inexpensive used in Kyoto gardens. Though most *kare sansui* gardens include symbolic elements, this one strives for an abstract beauty in harmony with the modern architecture and residential design of the building.

28. JIKŌ-IN
慈光院

865 Koizumi-chō, Yamato Kōriyama-shi, Nara 639-11
〒639-11　奈良県大和郡山市小泉町865

☎ 07435-3-3004

dry-landscape garden
early Edo period

HOURS: 8:00–5:00. Closed Wednesday.
ADMISSION FEE: ¥600 (including tea service).
PHOTOGRAPHY: Permitted.
BEST TIME TO VISIT: May and June, for the azaleas.

NOTE: The veranda of the structure here is extremely broad, allowing the building to visually extend into the garden. The garden "fence" is but a low hedge, so that the distant view is clearly visible and well-integrated into the design.

Beyond the gate at the top of a dimly lighted road mounting a low hill is the farmhouse-style villa of Sadamasa Katagiri (1605-73), lord of the Koizumi clan and adviser on the tea ceremony to the shogunal family. The style of the villa captures the quiet rustic mood admired by tea-ceremony masters. The design of the garden, which uses primarily stones and azaleas, is skillfully arranged to include the unexpected sight of the Yamato basin spreading out in front.

29. ICHIJŌDANI ASAKURA RESIDENCE
一乗谷朝倉氏　館跡庭園

Kidonouchi-chō, Fukui-shi, Fukui 910-21
〒910-21　福井県福井市城戸ノ内町
☎ 0776-41-2301

stone-and-pond garden
Muromachi period

FORMAL NAME: Asakura-shi Yakata Ato Teien.
HOURS: Always open.
ADMISSION FEE: None.
PHOTOGRAPHY: Permitted.
BEST TIME TO VISIT: Autumn.

NOTE: A very dynamic garden using large, rough boulders somewhat out of proportion to the pond: this is especially true at the Yudono garden, one of the four gardens that have been restored here. See page 40.

This garden lay buried underground for over four centuries and was unearthed only when postwar excavations revealed its stone groupings and the courses its streams had followed. Though it is not an extant garden in the strictest sense, the imagination enables us to reconstruct its ancient form and the people who moved about in it. Fortunately, aristocratic visitors have left diary descriptions of the garden and the parties and poetry readings held in it.

Garden of the Lower Villa at Shugakuin, Kyoto.

Pond at Tenryū-ji, Kyoto.

Path at Uraku Garden, Aichi.

Pond and stone garden at Chishaku-in, Kyoto.

30. KUWABARA RESIDENCE
桑原邸庭園

Ichinose, Kami-ishizumachi, Yorō-gun, Gifu 503-14
〒503-14 岐阜県養老郡上石津町一之瀬
☎ 05844-7-2603

stroll garden and tea garden
mid-Edo period

Not open to the general public.

NOTE: The site contains a pond in the shape of the character for "heart," a stroll garden, an artificial hill, and, off to one side, a tea garden. Trees include wisteria and some very old pines; the trimmed azalea clumps are particularly fine.

In the fifteenth and sixteenth centuries, when Japan was in a constant state of war and turmoil, a castle stood on this site; the owners of the house today are descendants of the lord of that castle who later abandoned their samurai status and decided to make their living from the land. Nonetheless, the gate house (in the style called *nagayamon*) strongly suggests a samurai residence. The garden is in front of the inner guest rooms. The pond, especially beautiful in autumn when the foliage is at its brilliant best, was created by damming a valley stream. The grove of immense cryptomeria cedars in the background hints at the long history of both house and garden.

31. URAKU GARDEN
有楽苑

Gomonsaki, Inuyama-shi, Aichi 484
〒484 愛知県犬山市御門先
☎ 0568-61-4608

tea garden
modern period

HOURS: 9:00–4:00 (December–February). 9:00–5:00 (March–November).
ADMISSION FEE: ¥500.
PHOTOGRAPHY: Permitted.
BEST TIME TO VISIT: Spring.

NOTE: An extensive tea garden with numerous stepping stones and composite pathways. See page 217.

Retiring from active life in 1617, the samurai and tea master Oda Uraku built a tea pavilion called the Jo-an in the precincts of the temple Kennin-ji, in Kyoto. Passing through the hands of many owners thereafter, the pavilion finally found a permanent resting place when it was rebuilt on the grounds of the Hotel Inuyama in Aichi Prefecture in 1971. On that occasion architect Horiguchi Sutemi, who was in charge of the project, designed a new garden to accompany the building. The use of naturally low pruned plants has resulted in a design of great dignity.

32. KENROKU-EN
兼六園

Kenroku-machi, Kanazawa-shi, Ishikawa 920
〒920 石川県金沢市兼六町
☎ 0762-21-5850

stroll garden
late Edo period

HOURS: 6:30–6:00 (March 16–May, September–October 15). 6:30–6:30 (July–August, October 16–March 15).
ADMISSION FEE: ¥100.
PHOTOGRAPHY: Permitted.

NOTE: A twisting stream matches the garden path. The large and small waterfalls, fountains, and beautifully crafted bridges give this garden the distinctive flavor of the culture of this region.

A garden for the lords of Kaga, the Kenroku-en was a place I loved to visit in my high school days. We used to sing school songs at the tops of our lungs there. Projecting over part of the pond, water for which is drawn from the distant mountains, is a pavilion where tea-ceremony meals (*kaiseki*) are served. The boughs of the pines are suspended by ropes attached to tall poles to prevent their breaking in the heavy snows that fall frequently in this region. In the past, this interesting technique was probably used elsewhere as well, but it now survives only at the Kenroku-en.

33. SHIMIZU-EN
清水園

Daiei-chō, Shibata-shi, Niigata 957
〒957 新潟県新発田市大栄町

☎ 02542–2–2659

stroll garden
early Edo period

HOURS: 9:00–4:30. Closed December 26–February.
ADMISSION FEE: ¥350.
PHOTOGRAPHY: Permitted.
BEST TIME TO VISIT: Spring, autumn.

NOTE: Five tea pavilions surround a pond in the shape of the character for "water." The garden is considered an example of the Kyoto style and takes as its theme the conventional "Eight Views of Ōmi" (near Lake Biwa), which was popular with the painters of the time. The large Shoin building dates to 1666.

As late as l950 the surrounding area was a quiet suburb, but today this villa for the lords of the Shibata clan—whose fief was in the cold part of Honshu called *yukiguni*, or Snow Country—stands in a bustling city. The garden is small and well cared for. On moonlit nights, young ladies hold moon-viewings, poetry readings, or other kinds of parties here; on Sundays, there are frequently tea ceremonies.

34. HAMA-RIKYŪ GARDEN
浜離宮

Hamarikyū teien, Chūō-ku, Tokyo 104
〒104 中央区浜離宮庭園

☎ 03–541–0200

stroll garden
early Edo period

HOURS: 9:00–4:00. Closed every Monday and December 29–January 3.
ADMISSION FEE: ¥200.
PHOTOGRAPHY: Permitted.
BEST TIME TO VISIT: Spring.

NOTE: General Grant stayed here and met with the emperor in 1895. The tea pavilions and plantings were severely damaged, first by the great earthquake of 1923, and then during the Second World War.

Though usually referred to as the Hama Detached Palace, this garden—now a public park—never accommodated members of the imperial family and includes no architecture that might have served such a purpose. It was actually once a villa of Tokugawa Tsunashige (1644–78) and was completed in 1679. Formerly the large pond was on Tokyo Bay, but it is now cut off from the salt tides by extensive land reclamation on the far side of the garden. The Hama-Rikyū Garden is a popular place for relaxation with people working in the numerous high-rise buildings around it.

35. RIKUGI-EN
六義園

6–16–3 Honkomagome, Bunkyō-ku, Tokyo 113
〒113 文京区本駒込 6–16–3

☎ 03–941–2222

stroll garden
early Edo period

HOURS: 9:00–4:00. Closed Monday and December 29–January 3.
ADMISSION FEE: ¥200.
PHOTOGRAPHY: Permitted.
BEST TIME TO VISIT: May, for the azaleas.

NOTE: A pond in the center of the site contains a large central island and, to the southwest, a Hōrai island. Artificial hills rise on the north, east, and west. The view from the eastern shore is considered the best.

The original appearance of this strolling garden is fairly well preserved. Now a public park, it was once a residence of the powerful lord Yanagisawa Yoshiyasu (1658–1714). Eighty-eight points around the pond are symbolic representations of places cited in classical Japanese literature. The rhythm achieved by alternating dark and bright zones, spacious and confined areas, and sunlit groves and mysterious forests produces virtually a musical effect.

36. KEIO PLAZA HOTEL
京王プラザホテル

2-2-1 Nishi Shinjuku, Shinjuku-ku, Tokyo 160
〒160 新宿区西新宿 2-2-1
☎ 03-344-0111

stone garden
modern period

HOURS: Always open.
ADMISSION FEE: None.
PHOTOGRAPHY: Permitted.

NOTE: A pedestrian "space," between the hotel and street, consisting of a pavement of cut stones and irregular troughs built into a slight incline. The atmosphere here is somewhat dark and brooding. Another part of the garden contains a castlelike wall of heavy stone with several mouths from which pour fresh cascades.

Designer Fukaya Kōki refuses to limit himself to the kinds of plants traditional in gardens of the Kyoto style; instead he uses a wide variety of inexpensive plants abundant in the Tokyo suburbs, and once used largely for fuel. The unpretentious design he has created with such plants, for one of the gardens of the Keio Plaza Hotel in western Tokyo, appeals to almost everyone who sees it.

37. NANKO PARK
南湖公園

Nanko, Shirakawa-shi, Fukushima 961
〒961 福島県白河市南湖
☎ 02482-2-1111

stroll garden
mid-Edo period

HOURS: Always open.
ADMISSION FEE: None.
PHOTOGRAPHY: Permitted.
BEST TIME TO VISIT: Spring, for cherry blossoms and azaleas.

NOTE: Cherries and maples have been brought in, and insects, including crickets and fireflies, inhabit the grounds to provide the proper seasonal atmosphere. On the northern slope by the pond stands the pavilion Kyōraku-tei.

Matsudaira Sadanobu (1758–1829), a feudal lord of such administrative skill and intelligence that not a single person died of hunger in his small fief of Shirakawa during the devastating Tenmei famine of 1783–87, later attained a post of tremendous power in the Tokugawa shogunate and built a number of villas with outstanding gardens in Edo. This one, in Shirakawa, is in the style of a garden for strolling and has a large pond with azaleas in profusion around it. The garden was open to the general populace, even in Sadanobu's day, and can thus be called Japan's first public park.

38. ACHI SHRINE
阿知神社

Honchō, Kurashiki-shi, Okayama 710
〒710 岡山県倉敷市本町
☎ 0864-25-4898

natural stone grouping
shrine: Muromachi period

HOURS: Always open.
ADMISSION FEE: None.
PHOTOGRAPHY: Permitted.

NOTE: The shrine here probably dates from the Muromachi period, but the stone grouping has been celebrated from ancient times. The stones do not make a garden in the formal sense, and the atmosphere that surrounds them is celebratory, in contrast to the sterner strains of Buddhist worship and contemplation that infuse Zen temple gardens.

About 700 years ago, the sea extended to the lower reaches of Tsurugata Hill (roughly 200 meters high), where the Takahashi River empties. At the Achi Shrine on the top of that hill is a group of stones still decorated today with sacred ropes (*shimenawa*) and regarded as objects of religious veneration. The stones are actually protruding tips of the granite composing the hill itself, and can be called an early prototype of later garden arrangements.

39. RAIKYŪ-JI
頼久寺

Raikyū-ji-chō, Takahashi-shi, Okayama 716

〒716 岡山県高梁市頼久寺町

☎ 08662-2-3516

dry-landscape garden
early Edo period

HOURS: 9:00–5:00.
ADMISSION FEE: ¥300.
PHOTOGRAPHY: Permitted.
BEST TIME TO VISIT: May, for the azaleas.

NOTE: The design of the pruned hedge here is said to be very "masculine," representing, it is thought, a writhing dragon. The garden also contains evocations of the crane and tortoise, and on the former is a vertical stone that echoes the view of distant Mount Atago behind.

Masses of pruned camellias between a grove of bamboo in the background and undulated banks of pruned azaleas in front are the major attraction of this temple garden. In 1501, when he was only twenty-two, Kobori Enshū (who had become lord of the nearby castle) lived in the Raikyū-ji and may have been the creator of this bold garden design.

40. KŌRAKU-EN
後楽園

1-5 Kōraku-en, Okayama-shi, Okayama 703

〒703 岡山県岡山市後楽園1-5

☎ 0862-72-1148

stroll garden
mid-Edo period

HOURS: 8:30–5:45 (April–September). 9:00–4:45 (October–March).
ADMISSION FEE: ¥200.
PHOTOGRAPHY: Permitted.
BEST TIME TO VISIT: Early April, for the cherry blossoms.

NOTE: Much of this garden was damaged during the war, although it has been rebuilt. The area around the pond is meant to suggest the "Eight Views of Ōmi," a standard theme derived from a Chinese model. (See also 33, above.)

Unlike the garden of the same name in Tokyo, which has suffered to some extent the effects of urbanization, the Kōraku-en in Okayama has maintained the scale and grandeur of a feudal lord's villa. Begun in 1687 and completed in three phases, the garden includes spacious lawns, streams, bridges, waterfalls, rest pavilions, buildings for the tea ceremony, and a Noh theater. It is said to have been created for Tsuda Nagatada, a retainer of the Ikeda clan.

41. JŌEI-JI
常栄寺

Miyanoshita, Yamaguchi-shi, Yamaguchi 753

〒753 山口県山口市宮野下

☎ 0839-22-2272

stone-and-pond garden
Muromachi period

HOURS: 8:00–5:30.
ADMISSION FEE: ¥200.
PHOTOGRAPHY: Permitted.
BEST TIME TO VISIT: Autumn.

NOTE: The consensus of many garden scholars is that the stones at Jōei-ji are consciously angular in opposition to the spread of lawn in which they sit, and that this kind of contrast in garden elements is extremely successful. See pages 40, 179.

The temple Jōei-ji was once a villa of the Ōuchi feudal lords. The fifteenth-century painter Sesshū Tōyō is said to have designed the garden here. A waterfall feeds the spacious pond, which is dotted with many stones. In the flat part of the garden is a *kare sansui* zone with a large number of stone groupings; azaleas increase the power of the composition.

42. KATSURA RESIDENCE
桂邸庭園

Tsukahara, Shimomigita, Hōfu-shi, Yamaguchi 747
☎ 0835–23–0583

〒747 山口県防府市下右田塚原

dry-landscape garden
late Edo period

Not open to the general public.

NOTE: A flamboyant use of stone in a gravel sea, very abstract and powerful.

The garden here was created in the early eighteenth century, when the main residence was built, for Katsura Tadahara—a samurai trained in poetry, the tea ceremony, and Zen Buddhism. Katsura had both the qualifications and the self-confidence to design a garden of his own. The stone groupings in the *kare sansui* garden, which is famous as a fine place for viewing the moon, are bold and powerful; the stones were selected with great freedom, possibly because the work was done far from the restraining cultural influences of the capital.

43. OZAKI RESIDENCE
尾崎邸庭園

Uno, Hawai-chō, Tōhaku-gun, Tottori 682-07
☎ 0858–35–2003

〒682-07 鳥取県東伯郡羽合町宇野

pond garden
mid-Edo period

Not open to the general public.

NOTE: The garden consists of a pond that enfolds the main building of the house. Many of the plantings here are from tropical climates. They were brought to this area by empty trading ships from the south and then left behind when the ships loaded up with goods to take back to their home countries.

Ozaki Masuzō is dead now, and I am deeply troubled for not having made a visit to his grave yet. I vividly recall sitting and talking with him for hours as we looked out at the stone groupings in his garden, the pond with its limpid waters, the trees along its banks (especially the red pines), and the "borrowed" green mountains visible over the wall.

44. ITOHARA RESIDENCE
絲原邸庭園

Yokota-chō, Nita-gun, Shimane 699-18
☎ 08545–2–2121

〒699-18 鳥取県仁多郡横田町

tea garden
late Edo period

Not open to the general public.

NOTE: Tea culture flourished in this region and produced many fine gardens. The stepping stones are set high to accommodate the heavy snowfalls in winter.

The Itohara family worked at manufacturing iron from iron sands drawn from a river before modern methods were developed. Their factory is gone now, but the house and garden remain in the valley. In the background is the hillside, and on the grounds there is a forest, waterfall, stepping stones, a stone lantern—it is the grandness of the concept that is notable here. When I went to visit, a group of people were holding a haiku-reading party in a rented room facing the garden. The mountains in this region have apparently produced culture as well as iron.

45. SENSHŪ-KAKU
旧千秋閣

1 chōme, Shironouchi-chō, Tokushima-shi, Tokushima 770
〒770 徳島県徳島市城之内町１丁目

☎ 0886-22-3086

stroll garden
Momoyama period

HOURS: 9:00–4:00. Closed December 29–January 1.
ADMISSION FEE: ¥50.
PHOTOGRAPHY: Permitted.

BEST TIME TO VISIT: Spring, autumn.
NOTE: Separate pond and dry-landscape areas are joined together into a garden for strolling.

The garden was originally created on the castle grounds in 1585, when the Hachisuka clan assumed control of Tokushima. The scale and boldness of the design, with its vast stones in auspicious tortoise and crane arrangements, a bridge of natural stone over 10 meters in length, and vigorous stone groupings on the shores of the pond, speak eloquently of the Hachisukas' pride in the victories that had put them in this position of power. Nothing of similar vigor is to be seen in the gardens of Kyoto temples. Where garden designs of the preceding period were dominated by the tastes of priests and aristocrats, the Senshū-kaku represents a period of transition in which the warrior class was the more important influence.

46. KAGAWA PREFECTURAL HALL
香川県庁舎

1-4-10 Banchō, Takamatsu-shi, Kagawa 760
〒760 香川県高松市番町 1-4-10
☎ 0878-31-1111

stone-and-pond garden
modern period

HOURS: Always open.
ADMISSION FEE: None.
PHOTOGRAPHY: Permitted.

NOTE: The garden is attached to a government office building and takes into account the needs of the citizenry. Most of the ground is open and flat, for easy assembly. In summer, the space can serve as a theater for the community's traditional dancing during the festival of Obon.

Local split granite is used in the stone groupings of this garden, which also includes a pond, lawns, and an artificial hillock. Architect Tange Kenzō created both the garden and the prefectural building itself. An element of chance dominates the aesthetics of the stone groups, since it is impossible to know for certain what shapes the stones will take when they are split. Traditional gardens relied always on natural stones of the kind found on beaches and in the beds of mountain rivers.

47. RITSURIN PARK
栗林園

1-20-16 Ritsurin-chō, Takamatsu-shi, Kagawa 760
〒760 香川県高松市栗林町 1-20-16
☎ 0878-33-7411

stroll garden
mid-Edo period

HOURS: 6:30–5:00 (November–February). 6:30–6:00 (March, October). 6:30–6:30 (April–September).
ADMISSION FEE: ¥150.
PHOTOGRAPHY: Permitted.
BEST TIME TO VISIT: April, October.

NOTE: Ritsurin Park covers over 700,000 square meters and contains half a dozen ponds. The best view is looking across the Nanko pond to the Engetsu bridge and beyond, but in general, throughout the park, the scenery and plantings are exceptionally lovely. See page 4.

Once a villa of the Matsudaira lords, the Ritsurin is now a park. The Kikugetsu-tei pavilion adjacent to the Nanko pond is well cared for, and the park in general is a fully equipped public facility. The stone groupings preserve most of their original appearance. Although replantings and repairs have inevitably been necessary, the greatest care has been taken to adhere to the styles of the 1670s, when garden construction was begun.

48. JŌJU-EN AT SUIZEN-JI
水前寺成趣園

8-1 Suizen-ji Kōen, Kumamoto-shi, Kumamoto 862
〒862 熊本県熊本市水前寺公園 8-1
☎ 0963-83-4233

stroll garden
early Edo period

HOURS: 7:00–6:00.
ADMISSION FEE: ¥100.
PHOTOGRAPHY: Permitted.
BEST TIME TO VISIT: May, October.

NOTE: A tour-de-force of garden sculpture, with many of the features of a dry landscape blown up into larger-scale representations. In the past a feature of the garden was the "borrowed" scenery in the distance, but this can no longer be seen.

The major attractions of this garden, on a site where a villa for the Hosokawa lords of Kumamoto once stood, are its large pond, spread with gravel and fed by the crystal-clear waters of a spring; its undulating lawns; and an artificial hillock island patterned on Mount Fuji. Though the model for the island is Japanese, the idea behind it is Taoist Chinese: the Islands of the Blessed where immortal sages dwell. The stepping stones set in the pond contribute to a mood of grandeur suitable to a feudal lord's garden.

49. HIRAYAMA RESIDENCE
平山邸庭園

6163 Kōri, Chiran-chō, Kawanabe-gun, Kagoshima 897-03
〒897-03 鹿児島県川辺郡知覧町郡 6163
☎ 09938-3-2039

trimmed-hedge garden
mid-Edo period

NOTE: The town of Chiran in this part of Kyushu was formerly part of the Satsuma domain under the control of the Shimazu family. This, the following Mori Residence, and a few other residences belonged to important Satsuma samurai and are still extant, ranged along either side of a wide road. At the Hirayama Residence, the rockwork in the garden is unusual in that it is nothing more than stone platforms for display, behind which is a huge trimmed hedge.

HOURS: Not fixed.
ADMISSION FEE: ¥200.
PHOTOGRAPHY: Permitted.
BEST TIME TO VISIT: May, for the azaleas.

The garden was created in the late eighteenth century, when the surrounding area was developed by samurai who settled in the villages and took up farming. The Hirayama family was of this stock. The outstanding element of the garden is a large area of pruned azaleas. In the past, the garden and house were open to the public when the flowers bloomed; a sign saying "Please feel free to come in and look" was hung up when the Hirayama family was out.

50. MORI RESIDENCE
森邸庭園

6354 Kōri, Chiran-chō, Kawanabe-gun, Kagoshima 897-03
〒897-03 鹿児島県川辺郡知覧町郡 6354
☎ 09938-3-3185

pond garden
mid-Edo period

HOURS: 9:00–5:00.
ADMISSION FEE: ¥200.
PHOTOGRAPHY: Permitted.
BEST TIME TO VISIT: Spring, autumn.

NOTE: The garden employs a two-step hedge. In front, black pine has been trimmed into decorative shapes, while in back there is a giant azalea representing a mountain range. This garden is more grand than the others because it occupies the prominent position closest to the main castle.

Though most of the other houses in this area have gardens made primarily of plants with some stone groupings, lanterns, and trees, the Mori Residence alone has a pond fed with mountain water, pure enough to drink. In this house, as at the Hirayama Residence, when the family was out a note was left on the covered veranda inviting anyone to visit the garden. Suspicions obviously never troubled the people in this part of the country in times gone by.

BIBLIOGRAPHY

Bring, Mitchell, and Wayembergh, Josse. *Japanese Gardens: Design and Meaning.* New York: McGraw Hill, 1981.

Conder, Josiah. *Landscape Gardening of Japan.* Reprint edition. New York: Dover, 1963.

Covell, Dr. Jon, and Yamada, Abbot Sōbin. *Zen at Daitoku-ji.* Tokyo and New York: Kodansha International, 1974.

Davidson, A. K. *The Art of Zen Gardens.* Los Angeles: J. P. Tarcher, 1983.

Engel, David. *Japanese Gardens for Today.* Tokyo and Rutland, Vt.: Tuttle, 1959.

Engel, Heinrich. *The Japanese House: A Tradition for Contemporary Architecture.* Tokyo and Rutland, Vt.: Tuttle, 1964.

Fujioka, Michio. *Japanese Residences and Gardens: A Tradition of Integration.* Photographs by Kazunori Tsunenari. Tokyo and New York: Kodansha International, 1982.

————. *Kyoto Country Retreats: The Shugakuin and Katsura Palaces.* Photographs by Shigeo Okamoto. Tokyo and New York: Kodansha International, 1983.

Futagawa, Yukio. *Traditional Japanese Houses.* Text by Teiji Itoh. Translated by Richard L. Gage. New York: Rizzoli, 1983.

Hayakawa, Masao. *The Garden Art of Japan.* Translated by Richard L. Gage. Heibonsha Survey of Japanese Art, vol. 28. New York and Tokyo: Weatherhill and Heibonsha, 1973.

Holborn, Mark. *The Ocean in the Sand—Japan: From Landscape to Garden.* Boulder, Colo.: Shambhala, 1978.

Hoover, Thomas. *Zen Culture.* London: Routledge and Kegan Paul, 1977.

Ishimoto, Yasuhiro. *Katsura: Tradition and Creation in Japanese Architecture.* Texts by Walter Gropius and Kenzo Tange. New Haven: Yale University Press, 1960.

Itoh, Teiji. *The Elegant Japanese House: Traditional Sukiya Architecture.* New York and Tokyo: Walker and Weatherhill, 1969.

————. *The Japanese Garden: An Approach to Nature.* Photographs by Takeji Iwamiya. New Haven: Yale University Press, 1972.

————. *Space and Illusion in the Japanese Garden.* Photographs by Sosei Kuzunishi. Translated and adapted by Ralph Friedrich and Masajiro Shimamura. New York and Tokyo: Weatherhill and Tankosha, 1973.

————. *Imperial Gardens of Japan.* Photographs by Takeji Iwamiya. 2nd edition. New York and Tokyo: Weatherhill and Tankosha, 1978.

———— and others, eds. *Katsura.* Tokyo: Shinken-chikusha, 1983.

Kuck, Loraine. *The World of the Japanese Garden: From Chinese Origins to Modern Landscape Art.* Photographs by Takeji Iwamiya. 2nd edition. New York and Tokyo: Walker and Weatherhill, 1968.

Naito, Akira. *Katsura: A Princely Retreat.* Photographs by Takeshi Nishikawa. Tokyo and New York: Kodansha International, 1977.

Nakane, Kinsaku. *Kyoto Gardens.* Osaka: Hoikusha, 1967.

Okakura, Kakuzo. *The Book of Tea.* Reprint edition. Tokyo and Rutland, Vt.: Tuttle, 1963.

Paine, Robert T., and Soper, Alexander C. *The Art and Architecture of Japan.* 3rd edition. New York: Penguin Books, 1981.

Rossbach, Sarah. *Feng Shui: The Chinese Art of Placement.* New York: E. P. Dutton, 1983.

Sakuteiki: The Book of the Garden, by Toshitsuna Tachibana. Translated by Shigemaru Shimoyama. Tokyo: Town and City Planners, 1976.

Seike, Kiyoshi; Masanobu, Kudō; and Engel, David H. *A Japanese Touch for Your Garden.* Tokyo and New York: Kodansha International, 1980.

Shigemori, Kanto. *Japanese Gardens: Islands of Serenity.* Tokyo: Japan Publications, 1971.

————. *The Japanese Courtyard Garden: Landscapes for Small Spaces.* Photographs by Katsuhiko Mizuno. New York and Tokyo: Weatherhill, 1981.

Suzuki, D. T. *Introduction to Zen Buddhism.* New York: Grove Press, 1964.

Tange, Kenzo. *Ise: Prototype of Japanese Architecture.* Boston: M.I.T. Press, 1962.

Tanaka, Sen'o. *The Tea Ceremony.* Tokyo and New York: Kodansha International, 1973.

Treib, Marc, and Herman, Ron. *A Guide to the Gardens of Kyoto.* Tokyo: Shufunotomo, 1980.

INDEX

Text references precede illustration references. Boldface entries refer to the detailed garden descriptions on pages 206–24. Page references to illustrations are italicized; a color plate on an unnumbered page is indicated by the page number of the caption followed by an asterisk.

CREDITS AND ACKNOWLEDGMENTS

PHOTOGRAPHERS

Hata Ryo: 38, 101, 148 (right), 150 (right).

Inoue Hiromichi: 5 (bottom), 18–19, 50–51, 53, 54–55, 58, 59, 90, 93, 94, 95, 96–97, 100, 102, 107, 108, 109, 110, 113, 115, 118–19, 127, 128–29, 131, 132, 133, 139, 140, 149 (left), 175 (top), 182 (top), 204, 208 (bottom), 211 (bottom), 212 (bottom), 214 (top), 215 (bottom), 216 (bottom), 221 (bottom).

Irie Taikichi: 4 (bottom), 10–11, 15, 25, 33 (top), 64–65, 73 (bottom), 77 (bottom), 79 (top), 173, 183 (top), 202–3, 209 (bottom), 210 (top), 213 (bottom).

Ishimoto Yasuhiro: 16–17, 35, 36 (left), 41, 42–43, 44–45, 46–47, 48, 49, 56–57, 62–63, 71 (right), 98–99, 114, 175 (bottom), 193, 194–95, 196, 209 (top), 211 (center), 212 (center), 214 (center) 221 (top).

Kinomoto Giichi: 9, 68, 189 (right), 197, 210 (center, bottom), 214 (bottom), 220 (bottom).

Kobayashi Kenji: 116–17.

Maki Naomi: 66–67, 86 (right), 87, 120–21, 122, 123, 124, 138 (left), 158, 159 (top), 181 (left), 218 (top), 219 (top), 222, 224 (center, bottom).

Matsumura Yoshiharu: 60–61, 69 (courtesy *Wafū kenchiku* magazine), 215 (top), 218 (center).

Motoki Seiichi: 149 (right).

Murai Osamu: 153, 166 (left), 220 (top).

Nishikawa Takeshi: 22–23, 85.

Nobuhara Osamu: 8, 24, 70, 125, 154–55, 156, 157, 159 (bottom), 160, 161 (bottom), 162–63, 164, 165, 180 (top), 190.

Noguchi Michio: 161 (top).

Ōhashi Haruzō: 126, 130, 168, 212 (top), 213 (center), 217, 219 (center), 220 (center).

Ōhashi Tomio: 167.

Okamoto Shigeo: 4 (top), 12–13, 14, 52, 89, 184 (bottom), 186 (top left), 198–99, 200–201, 206 (top), 207 (top, center), 216 (top), 218 (bottom), 219 (bottom), 221 (center), 223, 224 (top).

Takase Yoshio: 166 (right).

Tsunenari Kazunori: 20–21.

Watanabe Yoshio: 2.

Yano Tatehiko: 83.

ARTISTS AND ILLUSTRATORS

Ishiguro Sachiko: 141, 143, 144, 145.

Kojima Michio: 75, 79, 103, 104 (based on volume 3 of *Nishizawa Fumitaka shōron-shū*, by Nishizawa Fumitaka, published in 1976 by Sagami Shobō), 135 (top).

Ōtake Rika: 105 (based on *Sakutei-ki hisho*, by Hisatsune Shūji, published in 1979 by Seibundō Shinkōsha), 135, 142, 147.

Suzuki Yoshito: 27, 176, 180, 181, 182, 183, 186.

This book could not have been produced without the cooperation of many photographers, artists, and institutions. In addition to those persons listed above, the editors would especially like to thank:

Fukutake Yūji and the Dai-ichi Shuppan Center, for help with photographs and introductions.

Hisatsune Hiroko, for explaining the Saihō-ji screen on page 101, and Sotoike Takao, for allowing it to be reproduced.

Kitagaki Sōichirō, for information about the *Chikujō-zu byōbu* on page 177.

Nishizawa Fumitaka, for help preparing the map of Saihō-ji on page 104.

Sasaki Yasuo, for valuable material and friendly advice on gardens and gardening.

Seibundō Shinkōsha, for information.

Yoshijima Tadao, owner of the Takayama house on page 38.

Abbot Yamada Sōbin, for generously permitting photography of Shinju-an.

The editors also wish to thank the following temples, shrines, and institutions that granted permission to reproduce photographs or objects in their collections and provided information about them:

Dai Nippon Chadō Gakkai (Greater Japan Tea-Ceremony Society), for the photographs on pages 85 and 149 (right).

Furumine Shrine, for the photographs on pages 8, 24, 148 (right), 150 (right), and 190.

Hōryū-ji, for the Yume-tagae Kannon, page 75.

Imperial Household Agency, for the selection from the *Manyōshū*, page 72, and the scroll *Kasuga gongen reigen-ki*, page 178.

Kitano Shrine, for the scroll *Kitano tenjin engi*, pages 186–87.

Kubosō Memorial Museum of Arts, for the scroll *Komakurabe gyōkō emaki*, page 37.

Mushanokōjisenke Tea School, for the photograph on pages 128–29.

Nagoya City Museum, for the screen *Chikujō-zu byōbu*, page 177.

National Diet Library, for the map *Shugakuin kami shimo ochaya ezu*, page 88.

National Museum of Japanese History, for the screen *Daigo hanami-zu byōbu*, page 174.

Omotesenke Tea School, for the portrait of Sen no Rikyū, page 84, and the photographs on pages 127 and 130.

Shinju-an of Daitoku-ji, for the portrait *Ikkyū Sōjun zō*, page 134, and the calligraphy on pages 136 and 137.

Shōkō-ji, for the Seikai mandala, page 29.

Shōsō-in, for the Tōdai-ji vase, page 71.

Tokugawa Reimei-kai Foundation, for the scroll *Genji monogatari emaki*, page 188.

Tokyo National Museum, for the portrait of Ashikaga Yoshimasa, page 82; the painting by Sesshū, page 179; and the painting *Takao kanpu-zu*, page 185.

Urasenke Tea School, for the photographs on pages 86 (left), 126, 132, 149 (left), and 150 (left), and the print *Cha-no-yu nichinichi-gusa*, page 148.

Zenrin-ji, for the Taima mandala, page 78.

The Edo-period illustrations of gardens on pages 74, 81, 103, 146, 171, 184, 189 are from *Miyako rinsen meisho zue*, an illustrated guide to famous gardens in Kyoto, published in 1799. The half-title illustration on page 169 and the drawings of garden fences on page 187 are from *Ishigumi enjō yaegaki-den*, published in 1827. The half-title illustrations on pages 39, 91, 111, and 191 are from *Tsukiyama teizō-den*, an illustrated gardening manual, published in 1735. The half-title illustration on page 151 was prepared by the Design Section of Iwaki Zōen. The plan for the Hayashiya Residence on page 6 was taken from volume 4 of *Nihon no Teien*, published in 1980 by Kodansha. The plan of Ryōan-ji on page 172 is based on measurements taken by Shigemori Mirei in 1938. The Asahi Shinbun Photo Service kindly provided the photographs on pages 73 (top) and 76.

定価18,000円
in Japan